Kailash Manasarovar

Veena Sharma holds a Ph.D in African Studies. She was Head of the Swahili Service, External Services Division, All India Radio from 1979 to 2001. She has travelled extensively in Africa and other parts of the world, and is the author of *Folk Tales of East Africa.* Presently she is the Editor of *Africa Quarterly*, brought out by the ICCR (Indian Council for Cultural Relations), and Chairperson, Prajna Foundation for Cultural Interaction and Studies. Besides her abiding interest in Africa, Veena Sharma is also interested in Vedanta.

Other Titles

Archana Mishra	*Casting the Evil Eye*
Claudia Preckel	*Begums of Bhopal*
Dhananjaya Singh	*The House of Marwar*
E. Jaiwant Paul	*Baji Rao: The Warrior Peshwa*
E. Jaiwant Paul	*Rani of Jhansi: Lakshmi Bai*
Girish Chaturvedi	*Tansen*
Indira Menon	*The Madras Quartet: Women in Karnatak Music*
Irene Frain	*Phoolan*
Jagdish Chander Wadhawan	*Manto Naama: The Life of Saadat Hasan Manto*
Jeannine Auboyer	*Buddha*
John Lall	*Begam Samru: Fading Portrait in a Gilded Frame*
Jyoti Jafa	*Nurjahan*
K.M. George	*The Best of Thakazhi Sivasankara Pillai*
Krishna Datta	*Calcutta: A Cultural and Literary History*
Lord Meghnad Desai	*Nehru's Hero: Dilip Kumar*
Maj. Gen. Ian Cardozo	*Param Vir: Our Heroes in Battle*
Namita Gokhale	*Mountain Echoes: Reminiscences of Kumaoni Women*
Neelima Dalmia Adhar	*Father Dearest: The Life and Times of R.K. Dalmia*
Nina Epton	*Beloved Empress: Mumtaz Mahal*
Rachel Dwyer	*Yash Chopra: Fifty Years in Indian Cinema*
Ralph Russel	*The Famous Ghalib*
Rashna Imhasly-Gandhi	*Psychology of Love: Wisdom of Indian Mythology*
Sangeeta Datta	*Shyam Benegal*
Savita Devi	*Maa . . . Siddheshwari*
Sethu Ramaswamy	*Bride at Ten, Mother at Fifteen*
Sumati Mutatkar	*Shrikrishna Narayan Ratanjankar 'Sujan'*
Surjit Kaur	*Amongst the Sikhs: Reaching for the Stars*
V.S. Naravane (ed.)	*Devdas and Other Stories by Sarat Chandra Chatterji*

Forthcoming Titles

Greta Rana	*Jung Bahadur Rana*
Maj. Gen. R.P. Singh	*Sawai Man Singh II*

Kailash Manasarovar

A Sacred Journey

Veena Sharma

LOTUS COLLECTION
ROLI BOOKS

Lotus Collection

This edition first published in 2004
The Lotus Collection
An imprint of
Roli Books Pvt. Ltd.
M-75, G.K. II Market
New Delhi 110 048
Phones: ++91 (11) 2921 2271, 2921 2782
2921 0886, Fax: ++91 (11) 2921 7185
E-mail: roli@vsnl.com; Website: rolibooks.com
Also at
Varanasi, Agra, Jaipur and the Netherlands

Cover design: Sneha Pamneja

Photo credit: Pages 6, 11, National Museum, New Delhi.

ISBN: 81-7436-329-7
Rs 295

Typeset in Minion by Roli Books Pvt. Ltd. and
printed at Tan Prints (India) Pvt. Ltd., Jhajjar, Haryana

Contents

Acknowledgements

A journey and the meditation on it are endeavours that cannot be accomplished at an individual level. They call for direction and support from innumerable beings – those that existed in times gone by and those that continue to be. In my case it was my *diksha guru* Swami Venkatesananda and my *gurus* Swami Krishnananda and Swami Brahmananda who imperceptibly awakened the consciousness of the great journey of life and the auxiliary journeys that make up its totality. They removed a great deal of mental dross to make the experience meaningful. The teachings of Swami Prabuddhananda cleared a number of concepts and those of Pracharya Padmanabha Sharma enabled me to gain fresh insights into the meaning of many words and myths.

Lama Doboom Tulku, M.N. Deshpande and A.N. Tripathi provided valuable information about the cultural, archaeological and geological aspects of the Kailash-Manasarovar area. Mangalam, Anuj Chandra and Vikram and Gautam Sharma helped with care, in the physical preparations.

Many played a role at various stages in the writing of this manuscript – some wayfarers and some co-travellers, treading the same path. It is not possible to mention all but some of them are Kate Zeiss, Lakshmi Ananada and Kanchana Natarajan.

Before it reached the publisher, the editing of the manuscript was done with sensitivity and care by Aradhana Bisht.

Susetta Bozzi worked on some of the graphics with uncompromising meticulousness.

Uday Sahay, Divya Bhava, Madhavi Malhotra, Kumkum Bhushan, Swamis Narasimhulu, Nityananda, and Sarvamangalananda have helped in many ways towards the completion of this book.

Through this book I remember my mother and father who instilled in us, their progeny, a striving to reach the difficult and an aspiration for the valuable in life.

Preface

I had always felt an attraction for the gleaming images of Kailash because of their association with Shiva, the creator and destroyer of the universe. In my mind Kailash had remained a mythical mountain without a material form. I learnt that it was a mountain made of rock and rubble located on this earth, only when an acquaintance told me that he had travelled to Kailash as well as Manasarovar, the lake that exists near the holy mountain. I was even more thrilled to learn that it was located in Tibet, the legendary Shangri-La that had an air of mystery about it and seemed to hold within it secrets that were not known to the rest of the world. The knowledge that the mountain was real, seized my imagination and intensified into a powerful urge to go there. My desire to undertake the yatra was not a rationally planned idea. Rather, it was a deep-seated compulsion that demanded fulfilment.

I learnt that India had entered into an agreement with China to allow pilgrims from this country to make monitored treks to this most hallowed site. A number of groups (usually comprising 30 to 40 people) were sent out every year, between the middle of June and the end of September. One could apply and await selection by a lottery system; the applications received were far more than the number of people who could be accommodated. Then one had to go through various tests – chiefly medical – before a final list of yatris for a particular group was announced. I found that those who got selected and managed to pass the tests often considered themselves to be especially called upon by the Lord of Kailash to come and tread the sacred land.

Since time immemorial, pilgrims from India have crossed the Himalayan ranges and paid homage to this most venerated site. They travelled singly or in small groups without worrying about visas, permissions or selections. They stayed in villages along the way and relied on food and shelter provided by the local people. Some reached their destination; others perished along the way as they were unable to bear the cold, the altitude, the physical strain or the lack of adequate food. Giving up life on the way to the abode of Shiva was considered auspicious, as it opened the gates of heaven. And those who reached Kailash became eligible for moksha, the ultimate liberation from the cycle of birth and death. The yatra became a purificatory exercise that rendered the mind worthy of union with the Divine, the eternal. Generally, mendicants and *sadhus* undertook this journey. Others went on this pilgrimage only when their worldly duties were over and did not mind ending their lives in the pursuit of the holiest of the holy. Such people often left their homes telling their families that if they did not return for two years or so they should be taken for dead.

In 1962, the holy route from India to Tibet was closed due to political problems between India and China. For several years neither yatris nor traders could cross over. The villages along the Indian side suffered because the trade in wool and salt – a major source of income – dwindled. Many of the mountain people moved down to the plains in search of alternative occupations. The younger people looked for white-collar jobs with the government. Older ones, and sometimes children, remained in the villages in order to tend their small land holdings.

Due to the sanctity attached to Kailash and Manasarovar, a pact was made between the two countries in 1981, to allow Indians to undertake the journey on a regular basis. Pilgrims were granted special permission under a specific visa. After a gap of almost two decades, the mountain path leading into Tibet came alive again. Since then, a number of groups have been to the holy mountain and the lake. In contrast to the earlier yatras which were undertaken on the strength of faith and resilience alone, the pilgrimages are now well organized, and more safe. Food and shelter are provided at predetermined places by arrangement with the Kumaon Mandal Vikas Nigam. Medical checks during the selection process and along the route are designed to prevent fatalities. Armed guards and informed guides keep the yatris protected from dacoits and wild animals that endangered the lives of earlier pilgrims. Even so, not every one completes the sacred journey. The ruthless terrain and the rigour of sustained climbing in high altitudes take their toll. Some yatris are even sent back after a few days of trekking. Some reach the base of the holy mountain but are unable to perform the parikramas or circumambulations of the mountain and the lake, as the altitude becomes an insurmountable hurdle. There have also been instances of individuals lost in unforeseen blizzards.

The yatra is expensive, but those who are committed find the money somehow. Some pilgrims go for the sake of adventure, or for savouring the spectacular beauty of the region. But most are impelled by a quest for the spiritual or for fulfilling a religious ritual.

The majority of the yatris today are people engaged in worldly pursuits and most can afford the expense. Even so, the arduous journey is not without its impact on the mind. Once performed, the yatra becomes a part of one's being; it surfaces again and again on the mental landscape under different circumstances, unfolding layers of meaning that may not have been tapped during the rigour of the physical journey.

For me, the journey has been a continuing process; it has not yet ceased to reveal various hues and shades of meaning. The symbolism and the starkness of the sacred environs; travelling with people of different temperaments and acting as the group's liaison officer – all these created a special dynamic. In writing about it, I have trodden the abode of the Lord of the Mountain many times over since the physical journey was performed.

Shiva, Kailash and Tibet

> Holy places never had any beginning. They have been holy from the time they were discovered, strongly alive because of the invisible presences breathing through them. Man is amazed or fearful as he feels the vibrations of invisible power in the air . . .
>
> Giuseppe Tucci
> *Tibet: The Land of Snows*

Kailash is considered the holiest mountain on earth by a number of faiths and religions. Through millennia, monks, yogis and pilgrims from all over the world have braved unimaginable hardships to reach this abode of gods. Its exceptional isolation and the peculiar contours of black granite that give it the appearance of a Shivalinga, have caused Kailash to be venerated as a place that is both representative and emblematic of Shiva. For Hindus, a journey to Kailash is considered the ultimate yatra due to both the difficulty of reaching it and the level of sanctity attached to it.

Kailash in Sanskrit means that which gleams in water. The water that covers the peak in the form of snow is symbolic of flawless purity. The shifting light patterns on and around Kailash show the mountain in a myriad ways – as if to say it cannot be fitted into or confined to any form known to humans. The holy waters of Lake Manasarovar nearby are always permeated by its shimmering reflection. The rising spire of Kailash on the one hand and the deep abyss of Manasarovar on the other symbolize the togetherness of Shiva and Shakti, the changeless and the ever-changing, in a manner surpassing human imagination. It is an avowal of the fact that nature is the best architect of her own eternal and dynamic truths.

A mammoth *svayambhu* (self-manifested) linga, Kailash is not a shrine created by human ingenuity. It is an emblem of eternity that stands unperturbed – a silent witness to the surroundings while it remains omnipresent, permanent and independent. Even while some mountains around it have been formed and reformed, as though offering their very strata in oblation to this lord of mountains, Kailash has withstood the ravages of time. Alone, in the midst of several mountains it does not form a part of, or have a relationship with, a continuous range. This makes it possible to go around it for a view, or *darshan,* of it from all sides, and for all its multi-dimensional facets.

As a natural shrine, the antiquity of Kailash is not restricted to recorded history. Rather, it seems to be synchronous with that of its presiding deity, Shiva. Its primordial status has placed it beyond any scriptural or prophetic tradition. At no time did a prophet arise and proclaim the peak to be sacred. The vast empty desert around it appears to declare that here nature is striving to withdraw into its simplest point of origin, its sentient source.

Meru of the Universe

Kailash has been seen as Meru, the creative centre or the nodal point from which the universe takes form and spreads out.

The word Meru is drawn from the root words *mi* and *ru. Mi* literally means *that which measures.* The measure of the universe must be greater than the universe and also run through it like a measuring rod. The word *ru* stands for a great reverberating sound, a centrifugal vibration that spreads outward to congeal into perceptible matter leading to the appearance of the sensate universe. The two words unite to connote the coming together of the abstract static and the sensuous dynamic for creation to unfold.

The Universe

Vedic creation myths describe the universe as being made up of five elements – akasha *(space),* vayu *(air),* agni *(fire),* jala *(water), and* prithvi *(earth). The subtlest of these,* akasha, *is all pervasive and has the sole quality of sound manifesting as vibrations, which form the substratum and the substance of the universe. It can be visualized as standing at the head of the other elements as a nodal point, and at the same time be seen to pervade them.*

From the subtle undifferentiated energy arise other, more tangible, elements that can be perceived by different sense organs. Hence we have:

Elements	***Quality***	***Perceptible to***
Akasha	Sound	Ears
Vayu	Sound, touch	Ears, skin
Agni	Sound, touch, form	Ears, skin, eyes
Jala	Sound, touch, form, taste	Ears, skin, eyes, tongue
Prithvi	Sound, touch, form, taste, smell	Ears, skin, eyes tongue, nose

If akasha *as the pervasive energy were to be visualized as a rod of awareness running through the other elements, it could be given the status of Meru.*

In Shiva Sutras, Jaideva Singh writes:
To gain an experience of akasha in its undifferentiated form would be to experience the potential which holds within it the multifarious forms.

The conical and regular form of Kailash appropriately replicates Meru. Its isolated location on the roof of the world makes it a suitable symbol for representing the great abstraction that permeates and enlivens all creation. Though represented as a physical location, it actually connotes the spirit that is life-giving. The concept of Meru pervades Jain, Buddhist and Hindu iconographies alike, all of which represent it as a rod piercing the universe. John Snelling, in his exhaustive literary pilgrimage to Mount Kailash, *The Sacred Mountain*, writes of the Puranic representations which see Meru as 'the source of all life-giving waters of the world'. Meru is 'quite naturally the home and playground of the highest gods . . .' [1] As the centre, or source, it has both an external and a spiritual significance. Snelling goes on to say:

> Externally, in any world system, the Centre represents that one great fixed point against which all measures may be taken and relations drawn. It is like a great surveyor's rod at the heart of things, by its very presence giving coherence and form to that which would otherwise be incoherent and formless. It has the power, in short, to make cosmos out of chaos. It is also the most spiritual of places: indeed it is here that divine or spiritual reality impinges upon profane or mundane reality.
>
> Mount Meru appears to be the spearhead of what looks like a massive downward thrust of spiritual power or energy. This congeals into matter at the summit of the mountain, and thence proceeds downwards, diminishing as it goes, until it hits the terrestrial level, where it suddenly spins outwards, whirling a vortex of oceans and continents as far as the outer limits.[2]

In keeping with its divine attributes, Meru is imbued with fantastic qualities by the Puranas. Myth and geological fact are intermingled in these texts that are over 2000 years old. The ancients seem to have been aware of the cataclysmic subterranean movements that had taken place more than 60 million years ago, which resulted in the formation of continents and oceans as we see them today. The *Vishnu Purana* sees Meru as being 84,000 *yojanas* high and having a width of 32,000 *yojanas* (a *yojana* is equated to 14 kilometres).

> It is located in the middle of one of the seven continents that stand in concentric circles. These in turn are encircled by seven oceans of salty water and then seven seas of sweet water. Meru is golden in colour and is surrounded by lesser mountains which act as its support. The fruits of the trees around it keep the inhabitants free from old age and disease. The river Ganga falls upon it and dividing itself into four it flows in different directions. Divine beings inhabit the region.[3]

This description coincides with the geological explanation of the movement of tectonic plates under the surface of the earth. The continental plate called Gondwanaland collided with the northern Eurasian plate, pushing out the Tethyan Sea that separated the two plates. The sea was subducted under the northern plate. The collision compressed the surface of the plates and forced the crusts of both to rise, forming the highest plateau in the world. Kailash was created out of the debris that fell from the northern plate which formed the trans-Himalayan range. In fact, geologically, Meru as the centre and source of this activity, would lie further north of Kailash. But due to its peculiar positioning and the contours that have remained unchanged for millennia, Kailash came to be equated with Meru, the central rod around which universal bodies are perceived to rotate. Besides, Kailash is positioned just at the suture where the colliding continental plates became embedded into one another. It is here that the gases released from subterranean volcanic activity get released on to the surface of the earth.[4]

At the micro-cosmic level within the human body too, Meru is identified as the axial nerve centre in the form of the spinal column, the Meru *danda*, which is the repository of the life-giving spiritual essence. At the macro level, Meru figuratively represents a 'downflow' of the spirit which then spreads itself out in a multitude of sensate forms. At the micro level it shows the existence of this same energy in an impacted form at the basal level. From here it strives to ascend and connect to its subtler, more expansive levels. Thus transcending the world of division and limitation to experience the undifferentiated source, from the darkness of unknowing it strives to return to its subtle radiant form in the higher *chakras* located in the upper parts of the body.

Nada *and* Bindu

The entire universe comprising the movable and the immovable is of the nature of bindu *(dot) and* nada *(sound).* Bindu *is Shakti (power) and Shiva is the* nada. *Hence the universe is pervaded by Shiva and Shakti.* Bindu *is the support of* nada. *The universe has the support of* bindu. *Both* bindu *and* nada *together support the entire universe. The unification of* bindu *and* nada *is called* sakalikarana, *and the universe comes into existence as a result of this* sakalikarana.

As the original point from which creation spreads forth, Meru is also represented in the form of a *bindu*[5], a dense mass of sentient energy that pulsates with awareness. The linga, an icon for the abstract principle, contains within it the *bindu*, a symbol of creative energy. It is also a symbol of the *ardhanarishvara* form of Shiva which brings together the male and female aspects – the unchanging awareness and the dynamic ever-changing force – of creation.

Kailash and Shiva

Due to its peculiar contours, Kailash is seen not only as Meru but as a representation of Shiva in the form of a linga. A favoured god for many Hindus, Shiva is worshipped in various ways and forms for obtaining *salokya* (residence in his heavenly realm on Mount Kailash), *samipya* (nearness to him), *sarupya* (similarity with his auspicious and beautiful form and cosmic intellect) and *sayujya* (complete identity), which is equated to *moksha* (liberation from the recurring cycle of birth and death).[6] Held in awe as well as loving reverence, he is adored through iconographies that symbolize anthropomorphic form as well as abstraction. Whatever the mode of worship, those who obtain his blessing are bound to realize their goal. But even to receive his glance, his blessing is required. The *Shiva Purana* says, 'the full grandeur and greatness of Shivaloka (the realm of Shiva) can be known by anyone only out of the grace of Shiva and not otherwise . . .' It goes on to say:

> Those who come within His vision are certainly liberated. Peace is assured at the vision of Shiva. Shiva, the merciful, removes ignorance even as the sun removes all impurities and darkness by means of its rays. When ignorance is dispelled, the knowledge of Shiva begins to function.[7]

As a repository of paradoxical elements, Shiva fuses the contradictory qualities and polarities which constitute the universe. He encompasses destruction and creation, attraction and repulsion, awe and blessing, involution and evolution, immanence and transcendence. Yet, he himself, remains beyond them. When attributed with a human form, he is perceived as the greatest yogi who remains in eternal union with his consort, the Divine Shakti. As *nishprapancha,* the renunciate who possesses nothing, he remains indifferent to and unentangled in worldly affairs. Clad in a tiger or elephant skin, he smears ash from the *samshana* (cremation ground)

Above: The Kailash (North-east face).
Below: The Kailash (South-east face).

Line drawings of the Kailash by Sven Hedin. *Southern Tibet: 1906-1908,* vol. II, Lithographic Institute of the General Staff of the Swedish Army, Stockholm, 1917.

Shiva, the Serene One.

on his body. But he grants the boon of multifarious possessions to even the gods who reside in heaven. He is the slayer of Kama, the god of erotic love in Hindu mythology, yet he is the supreme lover and consort. His constancy in conjugal union is reflected in his recurring marriage to the Divine Energy that takes numerous forms to become united with him again and again. She represents birth and death while Shiva remains constant. She is born as Sati, the daughter of Daksha, a son of Brahma, the creator; and then as Parvati or Uma, the daughter of Himavan, the king of the Himalaya. In her second incarnation, as Parvati, she sheds her doubting nature and develops unwavering faith and an attitude of total surrender to permanently gain her rightful position by the side of Shiva. In all her incarnations She, the Shakti principle, seeks only Shiva while Shiva waits for her to reappear. Even the etymology of the word Shiva encapsulates both the eternal principle and the principle of change, which are personified as male and female. The letter 'sh' stands for the qualities of auspiciousness and excellence, which are constant, the vowel 'i' represents the changing principle, while the letter 'va' denotes the power to bring under control.[8]

Descent of Ganga

The descent of Ganga on earth was the result of long austerities performed by Bhagiratha, the great-great grandson of King Sagara. The sixty thousand sons of King Sagara were burnt to ashes by Kapil Muni whose wrath was aroused by their irreverential behaviour. Their ashes could be rejuvenated only if the waters of Ganga could be brought down to cleanse them. It took several generations before a person capable of pleasing Ganga (who resided in Heaven) was born. Bhagiratha pleased her by his penance. She agreed to come down to earth on the condition that Shiva would bear the fury of her waters. Ganga who is supposed to have been in love with Shiva wanted to be in proximity to him. Bhagiratha then prayed to Shiva who in his bounteousness agreed to bear her force. So when Ganga came down with all her destructive force, Shiva held her in his locks and walked off with her to Kailash. From there she divided herself into three streams. Two flowing to the east and west and the third following the chariot of Bhagiratha, who led her to the place where the ashes of his ancestors awaited rejuvenation so that they could go to heaven.

Mahabharata, *Vana Parva*, cantos 107, 108 and 109

Shiva is *ghora*, the terrible destroyer, but he also controls the great creative force which in the form of Ganga remains caught in his matted locks. The fire he holds in one hand annihilates even as it rejuvenates and purifies, for it converts

dross matter into subtle energy. As the creator of the universe he is *jyestha*, the most ancient, but as existent in everything that is born he is *sadyojata*, ever new. He is Nataraja, the Lord of Dance, who dances out the great drama of creation and destruction. While the dance represents the pulsations of cosmic rhythms and movements of time – past, present and future – the lifted toe of one foot points to a realm that lies beyond the physical plane and the three aspects of time. While apocalyptic devastation could result when Shiva decides to perform his cosmic dance, *tandava*, the vibrations set into motion by it lead to creation. Stella Kramrisch writes:

> The stamping of his foot, the gyrations of the body, his flailing arms toss the mountains into the air, the oceans rise, the stars are lashed and scattered by Shiva's matted hair. In order to save the world, Shiva in his perverse power dances the world out of existence wildly laughing, scattering ashes from his body so that the world may be renewed. This is the Tandava dance of Shiva as Kala-Mahakala, the Destroyer. But, from his flowing hair the rivers will flow again into existence and the rays of sun and moon will be seen again for what they are, the hair of Shiva.[9]

He plays the *damaru* (small drum), and its vibrations lead to the earliest sounds that emerge from the matrix of a sonic Absolute. They represent the fiery energy of speech, ascending through the phonemes of human vocalization to the transcendental realms of *nada*. *Nada* is the first vibration that crystallizes to form the perceptible universe. The first sensible manifestation in the great void, it represents the vortex of creativity and originality.

Shiva of the terrifying visage is also the most beautiful. His colour is like the burnished copper and red of the rising sun. He is *shanta*, the most serene and tranquil. As *neelkantha*, he is the saviour who contains in his throat the deadly *kalkuta* poison that would have destroyed the three worlds.

Neelkantha

When the gods and demons, for the sake of amrit, the divine nectar, churned the Great Ocean at the behest of Vishnu, one of the things that appeared from it was a deadly poison which could destroy the whole of creation. The devas ran to Shiva seated on Kailash, who in his glory took it upon himself to store the poison in his throat. His great yogic powers allowed him to keep it there – neither swallowing nor releasing it – so that the world might be protected. That is why his throat is depicted as blue in colour[10].

It is to avoid getting burnt from the great heat emitted by the poison that Shiva chooses to live in an icy place. The snakes that he wears around his neck are, among other things, a symbol of water and have a further cooling effect. The moon and the river Ganga he supports on his head are also symbols of coolness. He likes to be near water and is pleased when water is offered to him in oblation.

While residing on the high Kailash mountain he yet reaches out to the lowest of the low. He is the renegade who scoffs at the false pride of the socially exalted. In pompous and grandiose gatherings he appears in an emaciated skeletal form, almost naked, wearing a garland of skulls.

The Renegade

There is the story of Shiva going to wed Parvati, the daughter of Himavan, the king of the mountain, accompanied by his ganas. The ganas were a comical and grotesque conglomerate of beings – some with one eye; some one leg; others with distorted faces – all dressed as paupers and looking like social misfits and deviants (symbolically, they represent matter as contrasted to the spirit). This was a strategy to jolt the pride of Maina, the mother of Parvati. Having preconceived notions of goodness and social acceptance, Maina fainted upon seeing this procession but not before reprimanding her daughter for choosing such a strange husband. Only later did Shiva manifest his beautiful form showing that ugliness and beauty are facets of the same being.

Shiva Mahapurana, *Book III*

In another story he appears as an outcast before Adi Shankaracharya who, having been brought up with rigid ideas of caste, shuns him. Shiva, in the form of an untouchable, opens Shankara's mind to the ultimate knowledge in which social distinctions have no meaning.

He is the friend of the wretched and those who appear to be forgotten by the world. Before him everyone is stripped, 'pierced through the physical body of skin, blood and bone to the core, to the illusion of men's imagined selves, where he challenges the most basic assumptions of man's very humanity.'[11] While explaining the 'pleasing principle' by knowing which 'all living beings surmount worldly miseries', Shiva said to Sati, his divine consort: 'Attracted by devotion and as a result of its influence, O Goddess, I go even to the houses of the base-born and outcasts. There is no doubt about it.'[12]

He rides Nandi, the bull that stands for dharma and righteousness. As the controller of Nandi, he oversees the maintenance of divine order. In his *rudra,* angry form, he is destructive and frightening, but he is easily moved by the music of the *veena.*[13]

He is *ashutosha*, easy to please. When Ravana tried to lift Kailash, Shiva crushed his arms under the mountain by pressing it down with the toe of one foot. At that time Ravana sang praises to Shiva and played his veena, an art in which he was an adept. The sweet strains of his *yal*, or *veena*, pleased Shiva who graced him with a boon – a special sword crafted with his own hand. Even to those who unwittingly worship any of his forms, he provides great boons, sometimes to his own detriment.

The Naïve One

A number of stories are prevalent about the naïveté of Shiva as he grants boons without thought for his own welfare.

One such story relates to Bhasmasura, the demon who was infatuated by Parvati. Bhasmasura prayed to Shiva and was granted the boon of being able to turn into ashes any person on whose head he placed his hand. The first person he wanted to try it on was Shiva himself. There followed a chase – Shiva running ahead with Bhasmasura following close at his heels. The drama was brought to an end by the intervention of Vishnu. Assuming the form of a beautiful woman he began to dance, encouraging Bhasmasura to imitate the movements. During the dance Vishnu placed his hand on his own head, Bhasmasura did the same and turned to ashes.

Shiva's human representations do not in any way minimize the divine. As Stella Kramrisch writes, even though the 'anthropomorphic references bring the god nearer to human understanding, that likeness to man does not limit him by contingencies of the body or time or the imperfections of the human condition.'[14] In his abstract form he is the Eternal Lord, the Sadashiva (*sada*: always, eternal), the undifferentiated all-pervasive awareness that resides in the heart of all beings.

The Heart of all Beings

The Panchabrahma Upanishad states: 'That ether is Shiva, the infinite existence, nondual consciousness and unsurpassed bliss . . . This Shiva is the witness established in the hearts of all beings . . . and manifests himself to the seeker in accord with the strength of vision and degree of spiritual development attained by the seeker. Hence this Shiva is known as the heart of all beings and the liberator from the bonds of worldly existence.'

As the essence of things he is closest to everything, yet difficult to realize. For he is the subtlest of all selves. This self has no sign, or linga, to distinguish it – it is *lingavarjita*. And yet, it is represented by the linga, the omnidirectional symbol of the formless from which manifest time and space arise. Shiva first manifested himself as a column of radiant energy – a linga – to show Brahma and Vishnu that he was beyond creation and preservation as he included them in himself.

The *Shiva Purana* narrates the story of a competition between Brahma and Vishnu, in which both wanted to prove their greatness over the other. Appearing in the form of a linga, it was Shiva who shattered their pride and established himself as the Supreme Being. The luminous column of light representing Shiva's power came to be known as the Shivalinga. But he defied even that representation as he appeared to Brahma and Vishnu in his *saguna,* or human form, out of the radiant linga to establish that spirit and matter are not disparate elements but facets of the same Divinity. Hence the linga is sometimes represented as bearing the different faces of Shiva. Sometimes it is shown with five faces – four commanding the cardinal directions and one gazing upwards, beyond the material universe.

It is not out of character for such a deity to choose a residence that is *vishama,* difficult of access. His abode must remind believers of the vastness and absence of material form that go into an experience of Shiva. It must evoke a sense of the energy that may have preceded the creation of the universe.

Tibet

Like Shiva whose legendary abode it supports, western Tibet is also a tangle of sublime paradoxes. A vast desert, it is also the source of four mighty rivers – the Indus, Sutlej, Brahmaputra and Karnali. Two of these – the Indus and the Brahmaputra – embrace in their outstretched arms the whole width of the Indian subcontinent from west to east. The Indus has given the subcontinent the name by which it is popularly known. The capacity of this region to act as a watershed for the subcontinent is perhaps what has influenced Hindu myths to pronounce it to be the home of the sacred river Ganga. Tibetan myths also look upon it as the source of the Ganga, even when no geographical connection has been established between the holy river and this sanctified region. The iconic and mythical association of Ganga with Shiva could be one reason for the myth's insistence that the Ganga originates at Kailash.

Tibet is the home of two of the world's most sacred lakes, Manasarovar and Gauri Kund. The latter is believed to be the highest fresh water lake on earth. The desert which has almost no vegetation, supports creatures such as rabbits, kayaks or wild asses and the rare musk deer. The most prized souvenir that people bring from this desert plateau are stones embedded with fossils of fish. But organic life is not the most important part of Tibet's fascinating geography. The contours of the land itself give it the unique characteristics for which it has become known. Lama Anagarika writes:

> Organic life is reduced to a minimum and does not play any role in the formation and appearance of the landscape or interfere with its plastic purity, but the landscape itself appears like the organic expression of primeval forces. Bare mountains expose in far-swinging lines the fundamental laws of gravitation. The roles of heaven and earth are reversed. While normally the sky appears lighter than the landscape, the sky here is dark and deep while the landscape stands out against it in radiating colours, as if it were the source of light. Red and yellow rocks rise like flames against the dark blue and velvet curtain of the sky.
>
> Even the waters of the rivers and brooks rise and fall in accordance with this celestial rhythm, because during the twelve

> hours of daytime, the snow on the mountains melts due to the intensity of the sun's rays (in spite of the low temperature of the air), while at night it freezes again, so that the supply of water is stopped. But as it takes the water twelve hours on an average to come down from the mountains, the high tide of the rivers begins in the evening and ebbs in the morning. Often smaller water-courses dry out completely during the day and appear only at night, so that one who unknowingly pitches his tent in the dry bed of such a rivulet may suddenly be washed away at night by the rushing waters.[15]

Though cut off from the rest of the world by high mountain ranges, the desert plateau has attracted the attention of Hindus, Buddhists and Jains from all over the world. All their myths associate Kailash with important events in the lives of their most revered figures. For the Bons, followers of the pre-Buddhist shamanic religion of Tibet, it is the 'Nine-storey Swastika Mountain' which contains the mystic soul of the region. The Buddhists believe that the Buddha stepped on the mountain to keep it from being moved away by Ravana, a king of the netherworld (not to be confused with the king of Lanka in the *Ramayana*). For the Jains, Kailash remains a place where their first Tirthankara gained spiritual enlightenment.

While religious imagination imbues Kailash with a number of gods, goddesses, sages, divinities and magical beings, in fact it is 'an inhospitable waste of frozen desert, windswept and waterless, frightening and almost formidable in its geographical features . . . '[16] Yet it has frequently been visited by foreign pilgrims and travellers, some of whom – at the risk of their lives – disguised themselves as Hindu or Buddhist monks and braved the difficult route. Such people were often driven by curiosity and adventure.

Western Tibet supports geological phenomena found nowhere else on earth. The two continental plates collided in a manner that crunched the crusts of both and in the process pushed out the waters of a sea that separated them causing mountains to be created out of what was a sea bed. In other parts of the world, as at the southern tip of Latin America, the subterranean plates moved under water raising the altitude of the total land mass without causing cataclysmic changes on the surface of the earth.[17]

The word Tibet has its root in two Tibetan words: *to* meaning highland, and *bo* the name that Tibetans give to themselves.[18] Indians along the border call them Bhotias. Sanskrit texts use the word *Bhot* for them. The mean height of the region is more than 4,000 metres. An old Tibetan ninth-century song describes it as the 'centre of high snow mountains, the source of great rivers, a lofty country, a pure land.'

Perhaps because of their highly intimidating nature, the passes that lead from India into Tibet did not serve as gateways for invaders from either side.* Rather, each of these functioned as a threshold negotiated by scholars and pundits for the sake of acquiring spiritual knowledge and for translating sacred Indian texts into Tibetan. Seekers from Tibet came to India looking for Buddhist preceptors and managed to persuade them to visit their land and stay there to propagate the Canon. Western Tibet became a place of fervent activity during the tenth and eleventh centuries when Tibetan Buddhism underwent a period of regeneration and purification. Among the well-known teachers who travelled there from India were Padmasambhava and Atisha, an Indian monk of royal birth and the rector of the Vikramashila University in Bengal. Atisha lived in Tibet between A.D. 1038 and A.D. 1052, founding the Kadampa Order which preceded the contemporary Gelugpa Order.

---

* Through thousands of years of its recorded, and oft-times unrecorded history there is no single mention of an invasion from the north, nor is a large-scale expedition from the south known to have crossed the mountains, in search of unconquered lands. *The Younghusband Expedition* Parshottam Mehra.

Milarepa, a Tibetan ascetic, (whose great-grandguru was Naropa, a learned pundit from Kashmir) is also said to have done penance near Kailash. Milarepa went to Kailash in the year 1093 and had many theological debates and magical contests with the Bon shamanistic priest Naro Bonchung, defeating him each time. To establish the unchallenged supremacy of Buddhism in Tibet, it was necessary to appropriate the most sacred mountain and its environs. Milarepa was a follower of the Kargyu sect, of the 'black hat' lamas. This is why Kailash is specially visited by the followers of this sect.

For the Hindus, Kailash is both the abode and the emblem of Shiva. Despite differences in climate, geographical contours and ethnic background, India and Tibet developed an important link because of the sacred mountain. A number of Tibetan myths about the region incorporate Indian myths. The Tibetan language, which was unconnected to Sanskrit, developed a script drawn from Devanagari. The modes of worship, too, became a blend of Indian and Tibetan.

For Indian pilgrims, a journey to Kailash becomes a special experience that cannot but leave a lasting impact on their beings, shaping and altering their vision, perspective and consciousness. It is not for nothing that those who complete the journey are honoured and often given a special welcome on their return.

Yatra

> [A pilgrimage] carries its meaning in itself, by relying on an outer urge which operates on two planes: on the physical plane as well as on the spiritual plane. [It is] a movement not only in the outer, but equally in inner space, a movement whose spontaneity is that of the nature of all life, i.e., of all that grows continually beyond its momentary form, a movement that always starts from an invisible inner core.
>
> Lama Anagarika Govinda
> *The Way of the White Cloud*

Yatra is a ritual, a *vrata*, or an austerity, performed with a given end in view. It is a journey undertaken to reach a specific place where communion with a particular deity may be confirmed and celebrated. The apparent objective could be very mundane, such as the gaining of a better life in this world or the next. This immediate motive is subsumed by the larger idea of attaining moksha, liberation from the existential bond with the transient universe. The liberation is sought by discovering the eternal and unchanging principle, the spirit that is the substratum of the manifold sensory and external phenomena.

The urge to perform a yatra arises in the individual straining at the fetters of limitation – psychological, mental or physical. It is rooted in the human striving to enter an arena where perceptions of internal and external, subject and object, perceiver and perceived lose their demarcations to merge into a unified awareness. It is as though the yatra were a means for connecting with an inner truth that otherwise seems impenetrable. It becomes a bridge for connecting the multitudinous mundane to an undifferentiated truth that holds within it the potential for all that is manifest. So far as this truth is known to reside in the inner recesses of the heart, a yatra symbolizes a correlation between external bodily exertion and a discovery of the spirit.

The physical activity of yatra is combined with a psychological and spiritual progression which unfolds as the individual proceeds to the destination. While negotiating external space, the pilgrim is called upon to keep the mind focused on the spiritual or religious objective and abstain from distracting activities and thoughts. Keeping out extraneous thoughts develops conceptual clarity and strength of mind. Halting places along the way often act as markers where inner transformations take place. In a certain sense, traversing a pilgrim route may be equated to ascending the chakras, the energy centres along the spinal column in the human body. The chakras represent different levels of consciousness – ascending from those symbolizing the personalized ego to a recognition of one's non-individuated divinity. Psychological transformations along the way help to remove erroneous notions about oneself and one's relation to the universe. Through interaction with other pilgrims and a gradual erosion of preconceived ideas about position, wealth and sundry beliefs, a yatra puts one in touch with one's essential humanity. As one ploughs one's way through challenging and inhospitable terrains and situations, one discovers that it is strength of will that takes one through. Face to face with the elements in the raw, one may discover great internal resources and find support coming from unexpected and seemingly lowly sources.

Significance of Place

Traditionally, Indians have embarked on many difficult yatras and, in the process, found that some places radiate an elemental energy not felt elsewhere. In these nodes of energy, the presence of the Divine is felt more palpably than in places which buzz with mundane activity. Contact with the Divine is more easily made and reinforced in places where worldly distractions are at a minimum. Generally, the human mind has sought to experience its own core in the loneliest and the most desolate spots. In the words of Lama Anagarika Govinda: 'Solitude seems to produce a similar effect as certain meditational or yogic exercises: it automatically removes distraction by outer influences and thus creates a state of dwelling within oneself, a state of natural concentration.'[1]

Physically the journey culminates in a definite destination, a *tirtha sthana* or a place that enables one to 'cross over'. The symbolic crossing is from ignorance to knowledge, from mortality to immortality. The *tirtha sthana* holds a special significance either because it is associated with a religious event or it may have a special location which evokes an experience outside the dull and gross phenomena of daily life. It is usually a place that lifts the mind out of its limited functioning, stretching it to grasp new meanings. Many people have been known to break out into poetry or other creative endeavours that they had not considered themselves capable of.

Kailash and its surroundings vibrate with an unearthly energy where the transcendent and the immanent, the noumenon and phenomenon appear to fuse together in surreal complicity. It evokes an awe that stirs the mind to surrender and offer itself in oblation. Petty and disparate waves of thought subside when faced with the vastness that surrounds the spire of Kailash, which stands as a connecting link between heaven and earth, the ethereal and the terrestrial, the spiritual and the mundane, coalescing them into one unified whole.

Kailash is not a thing to be grasped by physical conquest or by intellectual progression. It can only be discovered. Its power resides in the individual's capacity to experience. And paradoxically, Kailash itself helps to sharpen that capacity. Even the most unbelieving who start out with the objective of undertaking an adventurous trek are touched by the mountain's stark grandeur. Sven Hedin, the Swedish explorer who travelled to Kailash in the early 1900s in search of the source of the Brahmaputra, wrote:

> Our wanderings round Kang-rinpoche, the 'holy ice mountain' or the 'ice jewel' is one of my most memorable recollections in Tibet, and I quite understand how the Tibetans can regard as a divine sanctuary this wonderful mountain which has so striking resemblance to a chorten, the monument which is erected in memory of a deceased saint within or without the temples. How often during our roaming have I heard of this mountain of salvation! And now I myself walked in pilgrim garb around the path between the monasteries, which are set like precious stones in a bangle, in the track of pilgrims round Kang-rinpoche, the finger which points up to the mighty gods throned like stars in unfathomable space.[2]

It was not Hedin's scientific work but his description of the place – 'a bare rocky countryside out of which the summit of a snow-clad mountain rose up like a glittering pyramid of silver' – that inspired young Herbert Tichy of the University of Vienna to undertake, in the 1930s, a journey to Kailash that caused him great hardship and difficulty. A geologist by profession, he too was greatly moved by the spirit and beauty of the mountain. John Snelling, who met the scientist in later years, writes of him:

> Despite the rigours that inexorable, primordial land had imposed upon him, the Austrian knew that it had worked a potent magic. The sheer scale of the landscape, its rarefied and impossible beauties would always linger in his memory, calling him back. And if he had any choice in the matter, he would choose to die within sight of Mount Kailash rather than anywhere else.[3]

For orthodox believers, the Kailash pilgrimage may turn out to be an experience that cuts through the straitjacket of beliefs. They may find themselves stripped of conventional notions as they open up to a supra-religious experience. The usual rituals that they are used to may appear trivial and meaningless in the presence of this great natural monument. Here they may unwittingly rid themselves of the need to *do* something as they lay themselves bare to a sense of *being* in the face of a larger presence. In a vastness where every atom seems permeated by the Divine it seems almost ridiculous to individually offer worship to an idol or pray for some minor gain. All perfomances for purification or propitiation of a particular deity become redundant in the all-encompassing space.

For Swami Sivananda of Rishikesh who undertook the Kailash yatra in the 1940s with five rupees in his pocket and an immeasurable quantity of faith, the significance of the journey lay

> in the fact that the devotee considers not the physical aspect of the place but the spiritual power it symbolizes and the Divine Presence that is manifested and felt through it . . . powerful spiritual currents enter and purify all the sheaths, gross and subtle, destroying *vasanas*, sensual and material desires, and *samskaras*, the residue of actions performed. *Tamas*, dullness and ignorance and *rajas*, restless activity, are reduced. The concentrated influence of *satva*, serenity, awakens the dormant spiritual tendencies.

His medical background did not allow him to overlook the physical impact of the journey. He writes:

> The heart is invigorated and strengthened. The whole cardio-vascular, nervous, pulmonary, alimentary systems are thoroughly overhauled and purified. The whole body is filled with fresh, oxygenated blood . . . you will not get any disease for a period of twelve years as you are charged with new electrons, new atoms, new cells, new molecules and new nuclei with renovated protoplasm.[4]

Swami Pranavananda who performed 25 circumambulations of the holy mountain and 23 of the sacred lake between 1928 and 1949, during different seasons, describes the visual impact of the lake:

> One such sight is a hundred times more effective, impressive, and sufficient to put one into a meditative mood than a series of artificial sermons, meditation classes, or speeches from a pulpit. So it is that our ancestors and rishis used to keep themselves in touch with Mother Nature to have a glimpse of the Grand Architect . . . one forgets himself for hours together gazing at the beauty, charm, and grandeur of the oceanic Lake, teeming with pairs of graceful swans here and there merrily tossing up and down the waves.[5]

Lama Anagarika Govinda, who also travelled extensively in the area, wrote:

> . . . here the connections with the world I had been familiar with were completely severed, and the physical effects of high altitude, climate, and living conditions greatly contributed to this change. The spiritual importance of this change is not lessened by explaining it on the basis of the physical reactions . . . rarefied air of high altitudes has similar effects as certain exercises of pranayama, because it compels us to regulate our breathing in a particular way, especially when climbing or walking long distances.[6]

Parikrama

The *parikrama,* or circumambulation, of the natural shrines forms an important part of the journey to Kailash and Manasarovar. The *Shiva Purana* says: 'There is no sin in the world which cannot be destroyed by circumambulation. Hence one should dispel all sins by circumambulation alone.'[7] For the Buddhists, the *parikrama* around Kailash is equivalent to going through a cycle of life and rebirth into a new life. Performed around a central point, the *parikrama* is also a recognition of the unifying force of the Divine that holds the cosmos together. It is symbolic of seeing a thing from every side, in its totality.

Above all, a *parikrama* encapsulates the idea of striking forth in a world of time, asserting one's will for action, only to surrender and return to the origin, the source, which is restful and quiet. The path of evolution, of becoming, naturally culminates and fulfils itself in the discovery of the inward movement – the path of return, of involution, where movement in time ceases, where time itself ceases. The non-moving central point is a reminder of that innermost core around which life revolves. Assertion into the world of time culminates in a return to quietude. The two together – the setting forth and the return – complete the circle.

The very undertaking of a pilgrimage is propitious, for the word yatra means 'that which protects the onward movement'. Being of a sacred nature, the journey is considered worthy of protection by the Divine.

The Selection

> Only those blessed by the Lord of Kailash can undertake to tread this Great Path.
>
> *Vayu Purana* (1.12)

'We have to send a message to headquarters about your safe arrival. May I mention the time as six o'clock, madam?' My eyes alight on an efficient-looking man as I stiffly stumble out of the bus. We are in Kausani. As I strive to balance myself on the gentle slope thickly carpeted with oily pine needles, he asks again, 'And what will the departure time for tomorrow morning be?' After the hectic pre-departure activity in Delhi this stranger's enquiry is the first palpable evidence of my role as a Liaison Officer.

'This way please.' It is the keeper of the tourist bungalow built by the Kumaon Mandal Vikas Nigam (KMVN) on the promontory of a hill. On clear days, we are told, one gets a spectacular view of the famous peaks – Trishul and Nanda

Devi – from this elevated location. The town with its little shops lies several hundred feet below. Seven of us, the female component of the group, are led into a large dormitory. The 22 men are accommodated in three rooms – two above and one adjacent to ours. Most of the 29 yatris are unknown to each other and seem somewhat distracted. Perhaps they are preoccupied with thoughts of the path ahead or are too tired and nervous or perhaps just confused by the numerous tasks that had to be completed before we left Delhi. We will be together for the next 31 days, traversing very difficult terrain, resolving our individual personalities into the physical effort demanded by journey. The strain on the physical and mental resources, and our responses to it, will prove to be a leveller of egos.

The majority of yatris in our group are sedentary, middle-aged people given to a comfortable, even lazy lifestyle. Most are over 50 years old; three are between 23 and 25. The group is made up of believers and non-believers, yatris and trekkers, wealthy businessmen and professionals of limited means, Tamilians and Andhraites, Gujaratis and Punjabis, Bengalis and Kannadigas. Though the majority are from Maharashtra, it is almost as though the complex, conflicting, irrepressible heterogeneity that makes up India is encapsulated in these 29. The lure of the journey and the determination to make it to the forbidden land – whatever the odds – is the single common denominator that runs through this motley crowd. The decision to undertake the yatra bespeaks an urge that transcends thoughts of physical comfort and convenience.

The euphoria and excitement of actually starting the journey is mingled with the need to adjust to the stark structure of the guesthouse. The drizzle that has accompanied us in the last half hour of our journey adds to the bleakness of the bungalow. Austere and long, our room consists of two parallel rows of five beds each. Outside, the mist has closed in on the legendary view of the peaks; everyone's spirits seem to be low. The tense preparation period, the anxiety of medical check-ups, the last-minute collection of vital rations, the rushed release of foreign exchange on a Saturday morning and a myriad other chores have left each of us exhausted and bewildered. It has been a long day since we left Delhi at three in the morning. Other than this, there is apprehension about the journey ahead. We have been warned about landslides and inclement weather which could become obstacles on our way.

It is also difficult to give up the comforts and social positions we are used to. Kiran, a retired official with an army background, is obviously used to having her way. She was annoyed about not getting the seat of her choice on the bus to Kausani. Here, she immediately chooses a bed and opens a book. It is hard to tell whether she is reading or just keeping aloof. Deepa, a housewife who had joined an earlier batch but was sent back on medical grounds after a few days of travel, busily looks through her baggage for lack of anything else to do. A young girl just potters around; she is one of the youngest in the group – coquettish, opinionated. She displays neither the penchant for adventure nor the yearning of a seeker, nor, for that matter, ritual religiosity. Yet she is part of our group. The oldest woman yatri, Bhairavi, is 71. She, too, is not propelled by a religious yearning. For her, this journey will prove to be another addition to the long list of international place names she rattles off with the facility of a *dhaba* boy who parrots the names of dishes faster than the unwary customer can hear. Chander, who had been the Liaison Officer for a previous yatra and had helped me with useful tips, had warned against the inclusion of such a traveller in the group. 'Try to get her deleted during the medical check-ups. And if she does get through, just keep on suggesting that she need not do the *parikramas* in Tibet. She will pose problems.' I feel that anyone who has made the effort to undertake the venture should be given a fair chance.

There is one couple who appear as though they would head the list of casualties during the medical check-up. Their flabby physiques make them look hypertensive and rheumatic. But they have passed the initial medical examination and now their jolly voices drown those of the others in the room upstairs.

Set in a bowl in the middle of high mountains, Kausani has gained the reputation of being a home for thinkers who have striven to delve into the sublime. The name is drawn from Kosi, a small river that originates at Bhatkota East above Kausani. It meets the Ram Ganga at Mandoli. There is nothing more soothing than a walk in this tranquil place. A museum dedicated to the famous Indian poet, Sumitranandan Pant, is located behind the little *halwai* shop that sells hot *jalebis* at the corner of the road. The door to the small building is closed as it is past five o'clock. The inscription on the lintel gives us an introduction to Pant's deep faith in human nature. It says that trees are beautiful, animals and birds are beautiful but the most beautiful thing in creation is the human being. Pant was an admirer of the beauty and goodness he found in human beings. Perhaps it was a reflection of the impact of the surroundings on his mind.

I have barely gone half a kilometre or so through the pine-scented air when Satyam, a young trekker from Tamil Nadu, joins me. We walk to Anasakti Ashram built on a hill. The approach to it from our side is over large tracts of slippery moss – my first introduction on this journey to the imperative of stepping carefully, watching one's course, measuring one's stride. The ashram is peaceful, the air bracing. Mahatma Gandhi wrote his commentary on the Bhagvad Gita here. The building now houses a *bhajan* hall and a lodging. A helipad nearby indicates that Kausani is a favoured haunt of VIPs.

Along the way, Satyam tells me how he joined this expensive yatra, by sheer chance. The selection itself came as a surprise, and then money became an obstacle. He tried to tap whatever financial sources he could think of and just as he was about to give up, a benign uncle appeared with help. There is a belief that one who is chosen to perform a yatra cannot be prevented. By the same token, one who is not called upon to go will find it impossible, despite all efforts. I cannot help thinking of Narendra, a resident of Delhi who had spoken to me enthusiastically regarding preparations for the yatra the night before we left. He could not join the yatra due to a delay of just half an hour. It was the last day of our briefing at South Block, the office of the External Affairs Ministry which processes the yatra documents. Our passports were sent to the Chinese embassy for a group visa (individual visas are not issued for the journey). Since it was a Friday, the Chinese official had decided to sit a bit longer to finish the job. But she would entertain documents till 2 p.m. only! Narendra rushed in breathing heavily just after the messenger had left South Block with the passports. The Indian official responsible for organizing our yatra did not want to request the Chinese to accept a passport that had come in late. So a pleading Narendra had to be left behind as the official remained adamant.

This deletion made the total number in the group go down to 29 – one short of the quota of thirty laid down by the Chinese. Recognizing the potential for earning foreign exchange through this yatra, the Chinese have stipulated a necessary minimum amount that must be paid at the other end, irrespective of the number of yatris. Payment in foreign exchange would have to be made for 30 when we reach Taklakot in Tibet. The deficit will have to be made up by all of us from the meagre amount of extra exchange allowed for the yatra. Now, even for practical reasons, we cannot afford to let any other person drop out. Medical checks are to be conducted all along the way on the Indian side. Anyone who displays signs of physical disability can be dropped.

Darkness sets in quickly here. It is as though the sun has suddenly slid behind a screen of mountains without allowing the long twilight associated with the plains during this season. We experience nature more closely as we move through the mountains unencumbered by mundane activities. The drizzle begins again as we walk back. It looks as though there is going to be a heavy downpour during the night.

We head for the stark dining hall in our bungalow. Some pilgrims are already there, looking a bit sulky. There had been trivial problems at the very start particularly on issues like seats in the bus. One or two yatris had actually stepped off the bus because they could not sit where they wanted. Luckily the KMVN, our host organization on the Indian side, had provided an extra taxi. It had become clear that keeping the group together would not be an easy task. Chander had told me that as soon as the yatra begins the members would divide themselves into little groups based on their distinctiveness, real or imaginary. Divisions happen quite spontaneously. They can be prompted by ethnic backgrounds, similarity of personalities or even grouses over the arrangements or the inadequacy of information. The young girl and Deepa travel as a duo. Tiwariji has found an audience for his spiritual dissemination in Narendra. The Bombay boys see themselves as different from the others. The old lady finds security in proximity to me.

After dinner I announce plans for the next day. This becomes a regular pattern. While in Delhi, we had allocated the general duties to be performed by various individuals. These included looking after our bags when they are loaded and unloaded, cooking food during the *parikramas* in Tibet (where there would be no kitchen arrangement), preparing lists of passports and other items at the required time, and numerous other tasks.

Back in our room, the air is dense with unspoken mental conversations unwittingly exhaled by the women yatris. Sleep proves elusive. I slip out to the verandah. The rain has stopped and the tall pines are quiet under the now starry sky. Their presence stills the mind. Delhi – 400 kilometres away and 2000 metres below – recedes into a distant reality. Somehow, journeys have a way of delinking the mind from the trivia of everyday life, setting it on a trail of exploration within. I have felt this in a bus, a plane or a train, and sometimes in foreign places. This may be because thought has nothing to peg itself on, as the scenery either hurtles past or is too new to be comprehensible. The external journey causes the mind to recede inward into its own recesses. That is perhaps why yogis and sanyasis undertake yatras as a part of their sadhana.

I think of the fortuitous circumstances that enabled me to join the yatra. My appointment as Liaison Officer was like a call from the sacred mountain itself. I had been kept on stand-by, as some other important officials who would be given preference over me, wished to go. So, when the official from the Ministry called one day and said, 'Guess what?' my heart had missed a beat. Would I go, he had asked. I had made intense supplications to the Lord of the Mountain and had been preparing myself for more than six months. There was a sense of certainty in my mind that the call would come. I was ready to go.

After being selected by the External Affairs Ministry, the papers were to be processed by my parent office. About eight days before departure an official informed me that I had not gone through the 'proper channel' – i.e., first seeking permission from my office and then applying – my request was likely to be denied. I tried to justify my position, but I saw that I faced an insensate wall. I also knew that after being selected as the Liaison Officer; I would not renege whatever the consequences. But then, imperceptibly, the Lord of Kailash intervened, and the sought-after permission came.

From the plains of north India we would be trekking across numerous Himalayan ranges to the 'roof of the world' almost five kilometres above sea level. Soon after my appointment, Chander suggested, 'You must start your constitutionals.'

'What should I be doing?' I asked with some trepidation, as I had never been athletically inclined.

'Take long walks and do some jogging. That is all.'

'When should I start?'

'Today. And do it in shoes and socks, the woollen ones that you will wear there. I wore mine out preparing for it in the dead of summer,' he said helpfully.

My near-archless feet complained in the beginning. Boredom set in as I walked briskly, some 80 to 90 minutes every day. Just then, subtly, a mantra emerged and engaged the mind. The sense of ennui faded away as the repeated sound became an instrument for generating and channelling energy. It kept the mind focused. I felt that *mantra* and *yatra* were both vehicles – one complementing the other. The structure and cadence, the intonation and combination of particular sounds make the mantra a bearer of a certain kind of energy. Its incantation sets into motion a resonance that touches the vitality flowing through the nerve channels. The external effort comes to be supported by an inner rhythm.

Our well-organized yatra is not nearly as fraught with danger as it was in the past. Eating and sleeping arrangements are taken care of by the KMVN; the camps are fixed. The sense of community combined with armed protection for the group makes the yatra safe from wild animals and dacoits. Even so, there are difficulties. The daily medical inspections by the doctor determine whether a yatri is to be allowed to proceed. Even after clearance one may find oneself unable to climb, as the altitude can prove to be a ruthless deterrent. No one can be sure of completing the yatra till it is actually done.

The present group has successfully gone through the initial trials. Some believe that they are selected with a particular group because that too is preordained. And this assumption cannot be easily challenged. Durga, a teacher from Calcutta, wished to go with her sister in an earlier batch; she failed the medical test. Yet she passed the test for this one, the very next batch!

The Sublime and the Mundane

The sacred and the profane do not occupy separate spaces. They are manifestations in the same field.

The time to leave Kausani for Dharchula has been fixed for five-thirty in the morning. The bulk of our baggage has been left atop the bus to save time. It has been raining nonstop through the night. Yatris who have not followed packing instructions may find their things soaking wet at the next halt. Some have not kept aside necessities for the stay at Kausani. Instructions, repeated at the briefings and listed in a booklet, have not been heeded.

The KMVN arrangements are almost clockwork. Tea is served at 4 a.m., but we leave at six because of the heavy downpour. The time-bound yatra demands that we reach our halts at more or less predetermined hours. There is little possibility for deviation as the group is to meet the preceding batch returning from Tibet, at the Lipu Lekh Pass on a particular date and time. The same Chinese and Tibetan guides who bring them up to the Pass will guide our group down into the Tibetan plateau.

The early morning schedules are met with some disgruntlement but no major fuss; at this point no one wishes to upset the harmony. Kalu Ram, the conscientious driver deputed by the KMVN, rents the morning mist and silence with his shrill horn. His brilliant fog lights vainly attempt to pierce the thick darkness. What matters to him is to get going and to off-load his passengers at their destination. And destinations are what we will be dealing with in the next 31 days.

A half-hour drive brings us to Bageshwar where we stop for breakfast. Bageshwar is located at the confluence of the Sarayu and Gomti rivers (not to be confused with the rivers of the same name lower down on the subcontinent). Confluences are considered sacred perhaps because rivers are considered holy; when two rivers come together the place becomes holier still. At this point rivers are often given a new name in which the identity of both gets merged. At Bageshwar, the two rivers join to form the Sharada. A number of religious melas and festivals dedicated to Devi are held here every year.

Bageshwar is mentioned as a holy place in the *Manas Khand* of the *Skanda Purana*. According to the *Skanda Purana*, Shiva appeared to sage Markandeya in the form of a *vyaghra,* leopard, in order to manipulate the release of the Sarayu river which had been held up here by the sage. *Vyaghra* in common parlance becomes *bagh*, from which arises the name of the place.

Several ancient Shiva temples stand along the edge of the river. In the middle of the Sarayu is a rock named Markandeya Shila, as the sage is said to have sat on it and performed *tapas.* It is believed that Markandeya, doomed to die at the age of 16, was able to avert impending death by severe penance. Shiva, the lord of time and death, appeared out of the linga before him and blessed him with the boon of eternal youth. Shiva does not just take life, He gives eternity as well.

Sage Markandeya is known to be the author of the *Devi Mahatmyam* (also called the *Durga Saptasati* because of the 700 *shlokas* that comprise it), a metaphorical text about the journey of the soul through various stages to its final destination of freedom, or moksha. It is a majestic description of the supreme effort in overcoming the lower psychological tendencies – from *tamas* to *rajas* and from *rajas* to *satva* and from there to final godhood. *Tamas*, *rajas* and *satva* represent the mental gradations to be overcome before a state of tranquility can be experienced. The *Devi Mahatmyam* identifies three stages in which major psychological transformations of outlook and attitude can occur in the mind of the seeker. The three obstacles to higher realization are *mala*, which stands for desire, anger and greed; *vikshepa*, the unsteadiess of mind that distracts it in many different directions; and finally, *agyana* or ignorance about one's real nature which is the cause of the first two. The threefold transformations are presided over by three deities known as Maha-Kali, Maha-Lakshmi and Maha-Saraswati.[1] A temple dedicated to Bhadra Kali is visible on a neighbouring hill where sage Sandilya performed penance. He is said to have composed the *Bhakti Sutras* here.

Our yatra is like a journey through these obstracles, each of which provides an opportunity for inner evolution. In my mind it comes to be visualized as an ascent through three chakras which represent stages in development along the spiritual path – the basal (*muladhara*), the middle (*manipur*) and the higher (*ajna*).

The holy town is crowded with dhabas catering to truck drivers and tourists. Tinsel souvenirs hang from little shops in the midst of diesel fumes that attack the nostrils. The walls of the ancient temples are splashed with hoardings of detergents and paint emulsion. The town serves as a base camp for treks to the Pindari and Sunderdunga glaciers. The serene mountains that surround this hot and crowded town seem to bear no relationship with it. It is as though two opposed entities coexist side by side – one natural, the other intervened by humans.

Perhaps this is an appropriate beginning for our yatra. No sooner have I thought this, that my first little adventure unfolds. My camera, which has not been working until now, nosedives into a heap of fresh dung as I sit down to tie my shoe laces. The long, exposed snout of the zoom lens is smeared. There go my visions of coming back with memorable pictures of the journey. But Sundaram comes to my rescue and tenderly consecrates the instrument with the waters of the Sarayu. I insert a fresh set of batteries and lo and behold the camera works!

This is my first experience of the coexistence of the sacred and the profane, the sublime and the mundane, something we will encounter at many places along the way. My mindset is fast being shaped. Are the two realms separate and distinct realities or are they manifestations of the same energy that pervades everything? Is it humans who interfere with the sublimity of the Divine and make it appear ordinary?

As we re-board the bus, I notice one head missing. A cursory survey reveals one of the younger yatris in a barber's shop nearby. Suhail from Mumbai has been particular about keeping his pate smooth and cannot resist a last run of the razor through the near-invisible stubble on his head. He wishes to leave all impurities behind; his next shave will only be performed after returning from the mountain. And that at half price for a Kailash-returnee, by the same devoted barber.

We journey through the peripheral ranges of the Himalaya, and in two and a half hours we are at Chaukori for lunch. The KMVN guesthouse is set amidst neat tea gardens and the compound is alive with colour and fragrance. We are here in August, when the floral exuberance invigorates the mind.

After lunch I get into the accompanying taxi that carries the overflow of passengers. The idea is to move ahead of the bus and get a clearance certificate from the Additional Divisional Magistrate (ADM) at Didihat before we enter the 'notified' area from Jauljibi onwards. Even Indian nationals cannot go past without prior permission. The lists of names, passport numbers, camera numbers, and the like are to be deposited with the ADM for security reasons. The process depends on the whims of the official-in-charge; it could take hours.

On the way, clouds part briefly before we reach Didihat. Luminous golden peaks rise in the distance as though floating in clouds. Fore-grounded by dark forested ranges they seem ethereal and unreal, as though a bit of heaven had decided to reveal itself.

Now a district headquarters, Didihat had traditionally been a place where merchants from adjoining areas brought their goods for sale on a prescribed day of the week. Wool and salt from Tibet was exchanged for grain here. It has now grown into a small town in which consumables brought from the city and woollen articles made in the area are available. The office of the ADM in a small barrack-like structure is on the periphery. Rudra and Kiran are car sick, so the driver brings them tea while I go to meet the ADM.

Mr Tiwari is a genial man. As his assistants prepare our clearance papers, he presents a detailed picture of the path right up to Lipu Pass. He, too, is lured by the mountains and has taken various routes leading up to the Pass. But he has not been to Tibet. At times a *darshan* of Kailash can be had from vantage points in India. By drawing a map of other routes, through the Mana and Niti passes, he provides a graphic view of our route and places it in its proper geographical perspective. Mana Pass, believed to be the route taken by the Pandavas under the guidance of Yudhishthira, is more difficult. As the legend goes, the Pandavas decided to walk up to heaven at the end of their earthly sojourn. Heaven must have been the equivalent of Kailash, for they went past Badrinath in the direction of Kailash. Their journey described in the *Mahabharata* was wrought with difficulties and only Yudhishthira, the most righteous of them reached the destination. All the others fell along the path, thus establishing the belief that only purest of heart can reach the abode of Shiva.

The route prescribed for us is the easiest. Our work with the ADM is completed much sooner than expected. We walk around Didihat and wait for the bus. Small shops stock almost everything—there are biscuits and detergents, mill-made cloth and cheap electrical goods. Fumes of diesel fill the air. A small restaurant is tucked in one corner. We notice a tree trunk with small steps roughly hewn into it, resting almost vertically against a building. It leads into the upper floor of a shop. Subroto and I buy a couple of shawls, earth-coloured, spun and woven from local materials. We get on with the journey the moment the bus arrives.

A few kilometres further down at Jauljibi, we are required to stop for an official check. We meet two cynical militiamen closeted in a khaki tent, erected by the roadside. Sitting behind dusty registers they do not see the point of noting down vehicle and passport numbers as they have no means of following a vehicle if an unauthorized one goes past them. They raise some unexpected, surly objections regarding the number of people in the bus and claim that we have six more than the list supplied to them. Surprised at their objection, we help them thumb through the soggy register only to discover that they have been looking at the wrong page.

Jauljibi draws its name from the word *jib* meaning tongue. As two streams come together here, the land between them takes on the appearance of a tongue. Our onward journey goes along the Gauri Ganga. Many rivers originating in the Himalaya are given the name Ganga. The forests on the mountains are like the matted hair of Shiva and since Ganga resides in his locks, perhaps she is seen to reside in every stream and water course. A Tibetan myth also corroborates this connection.

Tibetan Myth

The 60,000 sons of King Dugchen, great grandfather of King Bhagirath, were snatched and burnt to ashes by Khyabjug, who reigned under the sea. Bhagirath prayed to

Tsangpa, the king of gods who ordered Ganga to go down to the netherworld and rejuvenate them. But Ganga, being of high caste, did not want to go. Yet she could not disobey the king. So she devised a method: she would flow so fast that she would disappear underground. But Tsangpa knew her mind, so as punishment he imprisoned her in the hair of Wangchuk (another name for Shiva). Ganga tried to find the end of the hair but could not. So Bhagirath prayed again to Tsangpa who squeezed the hair of Wangchuk and brought out one drop of water, which fell on Mount Kailash. That divided itself into four – one became Tso Mapham, or Lake Manasarovar, from which the earthly Ganga originates, according to the myth.

Then Ganga decided to go to the Southern seas for which she had to cross the whole range of the Himalayas. On the way there was a Brahmin named Jahnu meditating in the Himalayas. Angered by the sound of this indisciplined, useless lady going through, disturbing him, he drank all her waters. Bhagirath now prayed again to please Jahnu, who released her from his ear. So, Ganga flowed into all four directions and down into the netherworld where she washed the ashes of the 60,000 sons of Dugchen and rejuvenated them.[2]

Rudra, his name bearing testimony to his preferred deity (it is one of the names of Shiva), is completely absorbed in chanting Shiva *stotras* – compositions in praise of the god – in a loving, melodious voice. It is only when his stomach revolts from time to time – the altitude and the hairpin bends make demands that his body is not used to – that he is jolted back into reality. We stop to enable him to breathe fresh mountain air and allow his stomach to settle.

Dharchula, on the banks of the Dhauli Ganga (the epithet Dhauli refers to its colour which is white), is a sultry town separated from 'Darchula' of Nepal by a suspension bridge across the foaming river. Our timely arrival at Dharchula provides an opportunity for many in the group to go to the other side and see a bit of 'foreign' land. There are no formalities to be completed for crossing from one side to the other. Phone calls to family and friends are made through the facilities available in Nepal. Payment is accepted in Indian rupees. Dharchula is another commercial centre where articles from the mountains are brought for sale. On the way back from Kailash, I walked the dusty streets, entered the homes of rich merchants, looking for old Tibetan carpets – all in vain. We saw a number of women at looms weaving thick piled rugs in garish colours and 'modern' designs. The velvety sheen and mellow colours of the traditional carpets were not to be found anywhere.

Surrounded by mountains, Dharchula has a hot and sticky climate. The logistics of our ascent and final decisions about the number of ponies and porters to be hired are to be worked out here. We are told we may find ourselves stranded since they will not be available further up. The extra money required and the enthusiasm for performing the yatra totally on foot are factors that prevent some from hiring ponies or porters. A set number for carrying the baggage have been hired by KMVN and paid for in Delhi. We need to hire some more for the extra baggage and for carrying some yatris' immediate requirements. It is possible that some of us may succumb to exhaustion midway and be incapable of walking further. After complicated calculations we arrive at an agreed number, only to discover later that animals and porters are available throughout the route. The yatras have given stimulus to a new occupation. Many hill-folk who had left the area have now returned with newly-acquired ponies and mules.

Satbir Singh, the leader of a group of five men provided by the Provincial Armoured Corps (PAC), introduces himself. We will be accompanied by these sturdy men in uniform all through our trek on the Indian side. The two KMVN guides, who will make our journey interesting with anecdotes and songs about the area, also join us here. Besides, there are two telecommunications men who carry walkie-talkies to remain in constant touch with 'headquarters'.

Our baggage is carefully weighed under the supervision of the sharp and dapper contractor responsible for its safe delivery to our various destinations along the route. Ratan Thapa, the stocky little man who can be spotted from a distance by the white Panama hat that never leaves his head, is a Bhotia from the village of Buddhi, almost midway between Dharchula and Lipu Pass. He belongs to a family that has seen good days, when trade in wool and salt between India and Tibet was brisk. At the beginning of the '60s the family was forced to change its business; now his brother runs a successful driving school in Dubai. Ratan came back from Dubai to look after business at home. His stocky frame marked by white sartorial elegance and an inscrutable flat-cheeked face is a reassuring presence.

We pay for the extra baggage from the common pool created for sundry expenses. This also takes care of the rations stocked in abundant quantities for use in Tibet. We determined the quantities through the wisdom gained by previous groups, and on the generosity of our co-yatris, none of whom want to starve on the desert plateau.

The final medical check-up also takes place here. Three or four people were tested repeatedly in Delhi for hypertension yet allowed to proceed. In Delhi, some found themselves placed on the threshold of a disability they were unaware of earlier; it made them nervous. Sandeep, a sturdy-looking young man and the biggest in size among us, was stumped by the information that his 'blood pressure level is on the brink'. He was asked to come for another check-up after a couple of days. None of the check-ups he had undergone *before* applying for the journey had shown any abnormality. He had not planned for extra days in Delhi. So he was obliged to travel back and forth between his hometown in Madhya Pradesh and Delhi a few times. More than that, the information burdened him with a sense of uncertainty. Would he make it? Every medical check-up finds him morose and anxious. The yatra throws up unexpected information at every turn. Determination will be needed to make it to the end.

The Sound of Mantra

Make a sacrificial stick of your body
Another stick from the sound of mantra
Rub these with the effort of intelligence
And realize the light within.

Adapted from *Kaivalya Upanishad*

The sound of rain pelting down on the tin roof of our dormitory, and the roar of the Dhauli Ganga below have kept us constant company during the night. It is a welcome change from city noise. Many of us have not slept much. We have spent long hours dividing common food items into separate parts for various stages of our journey. In Tibet the group will be divided into two for the performance of the two *parikramas*, one around Kailash and the other around the Manasarovar. Each group will have to carry its own rations during this period. The idea is to carry the minimum possible weight during each *parikrama* and to leave all else at the base camp.

Morning comes in the pouring rain. We load our luggage on to the bus with the help of torchlights, cover it with tarpaulin and depart in near darkness at six. Today we start our foot journey from Tawaghat, 17 kilometres ahead at an altitude of over 1200 metres. But right now, seated in the warm darkness of the bus we invoke Lord Shiva by chanting the *Mahamrityunjaya* and the *Panchakshri* mantras. The instruction booklet enjoins the yatris to make *Om Namah Shivaya* their slogan. I feel this is a trivialization of the radiant energy that makes up a mantra. The ancient teachers perceived the mantra to be a source of *tejas,* or energy which transforms mental substance into the spiritual. It is energy experienced as sound. The *Shiva Purana* seeks in mantra the nature of Shiva, which can be experienced by a devotee if it is intoned correctly and with intense concentration. The more an aspirant repeats the Shiva mantra, the greater is the presence of the God in her being.[1]

In the *Shiva Sutras* too, the mantra is seen to be of great importance in identifying with Shiva. Intent on the awareness of the deity inherent in the mantra, the devotee acquires identitification with that deity.[2] Etymologically, the word mantra is a combination of *manana*, pondering over the highest light of the I-consciousness, and *trana*, protection from transient existence. Besides, the repetition breaks the mind's habit of losing itself in a chain of thoughts and helps it to focus, thus awakening dormant psychic powers. We will be chanting the *panchakshri* mantra regularly, together and individually. Believer and non-believer become united and the fervent desire to reach the goal melts us all into one sonic bond.

My thoughts are interrupted by more prosaic matters at hand. The heavy rain has swept away the road. The group of yatris that preceded us, we are told, had to wade through an eight-kilometre stretch of raging monsoon rivulets, as their bus could not go up to the appointed place. They had to cross one of the torrential mountain streams using a rope bridge, as the original one had been washed away. The bridge has now been repaired, so our bus will be able to go over it.

The bus lurches on the dirt road that has been hastily cleared of massive landslides. Narrow, precarious passages allow it to pass, but a slight miscalculation could plunge us into the turbulent waters of the river in spate, more than a thousand feet below. The bus steers across waterfalls that cut through the mountain and rush past the road to meet the river below. Our driver negotiates loose rocks and whirling waters with skill and intrepidity. The sound of *Om Namah Shivaya* rises every time we go over a landslide or a watery obstacle. The Lord of Kailash will be invoked time and again – in distress and in joy. It is He, the deity of an almost unreachable abode, who has invited us here. He must clear our way. Our faith is strong. It is this deeply-felt force that will guide us and lend strength to our physical efforts.

We are headed directly north. The view is spectacular. Deep ravines on one side and towering mountains on the other imbue the landscape with a rugged and awe-inspiring beauty. The rain has not only made the greenery on the slopes fresh and lush, it has also inspired a variety show of waterfalls. On our side of the mountain these are charged with thunderous energy, pounding the river surface as they fall in a deafening curtain. On the other side, across the river, they look like delicate sprays etched out with a dry brush. This wondrous display of water over a stretch of about ten kilometres is like seeing the dance of Shiva in its creative and destructive aspects. Nature has unfolded her infinite variety in this area. The surroundings engross the mind and keep it from distracting thoughts.

Tawaghat is our last motorable point. A road is being constructed which will take future yatris up to the next camp at Pangu, but for us this is where we start our journey on foot. The rain stops and daylight spreads itself on the mountain slopes. It is warm and humid. The now slender Dhauli meets the Kali Ganga, the river we are to follow. The excitement of starting the trek has not prepared us for the pandemonium we encounter here. The odour of pony and mule dung pervades the morning air. In the midst of restive animals, rugged ponywallahs jostle and push each other to attract clients. The availability of a larger than the required number of animals and porters leads to near chaos. We have to snatch back our bags from aggressive, unsolicited porters. The contractor's help is finally sought to quieten the melee. Packets of breakfast provided by the KMVN are handed out to each yatri over the heads of jockeying porters and the caravan begins to move, but not before a resounding *Kailashpati Mahadeva ki Jaya* (Glory to the auspicious Lord of Kailash) is voiced.

As I wait to ensure that everyone has started off, I notice Kiran standing on one side, looking irritated. Her mule man is not there. 'I am not going to budge until he walks with me. I have hired him and I do not see why I should walk ahead while he trails somewhere behind.' Sandeep, in charge of keeping tabs on the porters and mule owners, looks on wearily, a hint of annoyance crossing his face. The general confusion at Tawaghat compounded by the anxiety of the travellers has tried his patience. The personal characteristics of each individual are beginning to etch themselves out on the general contours of the group even before we have started our trek. Recognizing them and living with these quirks will be a part of the discipline required. Relax, says a voice within me. 'Do not allow your own inner equilibrium to be disturbed.' It is a mantra I will be repeating often in the days to come. Finally, things are sorted out and we commence our trek.

The name Tawaghat probably comes from the shape of this embankment which is like a 'tawa', a flat griddle for making chapatis. From Tawaghat to Thani, our next pit stop, we have to climb 1,000 metres in a stretch of about one kilometre. The toughness of the ascent has given it the label *thanedar ki chaddhai,* or the police sub-inspector's climb! Yatris appear and disappear as they manoeuvre the sharp hairpin bends on the mountain path. The only redeeming factor of this lung-testing walk is that it affords one the satisfaction of looking down at the Kali to guage the amazing height we have reached.

The name Kali comes from the colour of the dark water. It also evokes the image of Goddess Kali, who has a turbulent temperament and governs time and death. She is one of the forms of Shakti, the consort of Shiva. Since time immemorial, pilgrims have sought out narrow passages along the rim of deep gorges whose raging waters cut through insurmountable ranges. While some mountains have disintegrated to form new ones, the rivers have continued in their original form and remain the most ancient denizens of the rugged region.

Dr Pandey from the KMVN walks with me. He is also journeying this path for the first time, and he will remain with us on the Indian side of our yatra. It is necessary to make stops at appropriate intervals and replenish lost fluids, he insists. One does not quite realize the extent to which the body is taxed in the mountains, he says. I cannot help thinking of a good friend who recently went into a deep coma and had to remain in an oxygen tent in Lhasa due to cerebral oedema caused by a little negligence. Snatches of instructions received from various sources surface in the mind: 'Do not walk too fast. Save your lungs for later as they will be put to greater tests in high altitudes. Caution all yatris to watch for changes in their own systems and visible signs of change in others. Negligence in the mountains can exact a heavy price.'

As we slowly wind our way upward, Man Singh, the ponywallah, informs us that the weather in this area is unpredictable. Punctuated with heavy breathing and the tinkle of large bells tied around the animals' necks, he relates the story of an earlier group some years ago. They were caught in a snow blizzard at the Lipu Pass and one man was lost due to the low visibility. His frozen body was brought down later by the Indo-Tibetan Border Police. His wife and daughter were subsequently allowed to visit the place where he lost his life.

Tripathiji, a well-intentioned co-yatri, tells me that he had written out his will before leaving. I am not the only whimsical one I realize, having written a statement to be handed over to my sons in case I did not return. Even though arrangements are much better now than they used to be, neither the elements nor one's bodily responses can be taken for granted. The possibility of a final end lurking in the mountain crevices gives a sharper edge and heightened awareness to the experience.

There is not much habitation on this steep incline nor much tree cover, and we feel the full force of the direct mountain sun. We see the tin-roofed structures at Tawaghat below getting smaller. Terraced green fields in the territory of Nepal are visible across the gorge of the Kali. We do not see any high mountain ranges as we are still in the lower foothills. The gorge of Kali enables us to see the depths to which it is possible to descend.

At Thani, we find a little shop where we can sit for a hot cup of tea. Many of us have taken up to two hours to get here. Some open their breakfast packets. Man Singh downs a plateful of freshly-cooked dried peas. In the days to come we will look forward to the delicacies of dried peas or red beans—the staple fare in every shop along the way. The make-shift shops that come up during the yatra season provide a pleasant break and enable yatris who walk at their own pace to come together.

The four-kilometre walk from Thani to Pangu is quite flat. Despite my desire to perform the yatra on foot, I decide to ride for a short distance. I peer down at the valleys and the sheer drops; it is wonderfully surprising to find that I am not frightened. Perhaps I anticipated the yatra so intensely that now all fears and misgivings have subsided. In fact, I am actually enjoying the ride. The freedom from the strain of walking allows me to take in the surroundings without distraction. Man Singh teaches me the technicalities of riding: how to maintain balance without clinging to the animal, how to manipulate the reins so as to get Samli, the mule, to obey without difficulty and so on. The short ride is useful as in Tibet we will have to handle horses without the help of ponywallahs.

We are greeted by the KMVN staff with a cool, much-needed drink when we reach the camp at Pangu. The fast walkers among us had already reached. Others are awaited. It is a glorious afternoon, with hours of sunlight still left for us to explore the surroundings.

The camp is a tin-roofed, make-shift structure overlooking the village of Pangu. Terraced fields of corn and beans add colour and charm to the landscape. In the distance we can hear the sound of a school bell. For a while we have moved away from the gorge of the Kali. There is peace in just listening to the muted motions of this remote village – children's voices mingled with the gurgle of Jyoti Nallah, a stream that flows through the village. Rudram collects a group of school children around him and teaches them some Shiva *stotras*. This is his first time away from home, and he misses the daily music lessons he gives his daughter. He becomes motivated and emotional when anyone shows interest in learning.

Lunch is served in a tiny verandah about as large as the table which accommodates the dishes. We sit on the stone boundary wall enjoying the sun and the open scenery as we eat. The village is spread out below. The KMVN manager of this camp explains how they labour over the menu for each group in advance so that every camp along the way may serve something different. If it is *chana* and rice here, the next one will provide beans, and the next *dal*. In the difficult conditions where all amenities must be transported by mules or porters over great distances, the lack of provisions needs to be made up by the warmth and friendliness of those in charge. 'We are not unaware of the psychological factor. If we meet you with a smile at the gate, half your tiredness will be forgotten,' he goes on to say. They perform their assignments with *shraddha bhava*, a feeling of devotion, as they see themselves performing their yatra through us, he says. Yatras need not always be undertaken personally. Serving yatris has its own significance. It is the attitude and generosity of people like him that makes the yatra even more worthwhile.

An adjoining verandah serves as the group's medical centre. There is the usual tension before the check-up. Ghanshyam who is a dentist and claims to treat his patients with the aid of hypnosis does his bit to help. Others lighten the mood with anecdotes to enable the tense ones to relax. All go through the test successfully.

Taking advantage of a moment of solitude, I sit on a rock promontory above a moss-covered, deserted temple. I wonder why it has been abandoned, trying to imagine its glory when it had its share of devotees. It stands in the middle of tall, graceful deodars that shade it from sunlight and give it a mysterious aura. The surrounding stillness and silence allow inner thoughts to surface. Some yatris are writing their diaries. Some are writing long letters to family and friends, sharing and recording their experiences. A few like Tripathiji are overwhelmed with emotion. He tells me how he became interested in spirituality. A refugee orphan from Pakistan, he survived and prospered by dint of his effort. But it was confrontation with losses that made him turn inward and look for the meaning of life. 'If a person is so preoccupied with the loss of material goods, what is life worth?' he pondered. At that point he met the man who is now his Guru. He sees his yatra as a call from Shiva, who has specially chosen him to come to his abode. A devoted man, Tripathiji has the air of one who bears the responsibility of instructing others. I am slowly getting to know the mindset of my co-travellers even as I explore my own. In this moment of quietude, I feel overtaken by a sense of gratitude for the Lord of the Mountain who has allowed me to approach him.

Over Bridges and Rivulets

What looks like individual accomplishment is actually made up of the efforts and energies of many.

The unpredictable mountain weather is something many of us are yet to get accustomed to. After the bright sunshine of the day, the camp's asbestos roof has been pelted with unrelenting rain through the night. For some of us it has been quite a novel experience to spend the night in a sleeping bag on the hard floor. The creepy-crawlies that shared the bag with me did not allow me much rest. We manage to leave at 6.30 just as a ray of light begins to pierce the mist. Packets of breakfast are handed out, and the yatris start stepping out gingerly on the wet, mossy path that leads from the camp down to the village.

The village of Pangu with its neat mud-plastered houses looks freshly washed. Old wrinkled faces peer at us with curiosity and mumble *Om Namah Shivaya* as we file past. Round-faced children chorus the mantra with folded hands.

Some yatris, in search of salvation, extend charity into their hands. Will it be long before the children begin expecting a toll from every passer-by?

The leisurely walk takes us past a variety of houses. Some have intricately carved wooden doors – a sign not only of aesthetic sensitivity but of a bygone era of prosperity. The double-storeyed houses are tall, narrow structures with small square windows set at high levels. Now and then, I observe a pair of eyes set in a furrowed, inscrutable face framed in a window. Pilgrim-watching makes a good pastime during hours of idleness. One gnarled old face looking down from an upper-story window quickly turns away when my eye meets it.

Prosperous-looking steel cupboards are visible through the open doors of some cement structures. Man Singh says they belong to the wealthy merchants whose business collapsed with the discontinuation of trade with Tibet. Now the older people who remain tend small patches of land while the younger ones live in the plains. Many are in the civil services and posted in various parts of the country, but the roots of the older ones are in these hills.

We reach Sosa by nine and hope to meet the group that is now on its way back. Useful tips with regard to the do's and don'ts in Tibet are expected from those returning. By now a tea break is also welcome. There are as usual one or two small shops. Opening up breakfast packets and energy supplements is becoming a mid-walk ritual. The protein supplements that I have keep me connected to Vikram who had sent them before the yatra. The collective concern and energies of family, friends and well wishers is a part of the yatra. Anuj, with his newly acquired medical degree, ensured that I carry adequate quantities of electral and glucose for myself and others. He and I had assiduously gone through a list of ailments – cerebral and pulmonary oedema, mountain sickness and others – possible at high altitudes. Kanchana and Gautam gave moral support through prayer. Mangalam inscribed an invocation to Ganesha, the god who wards off obstacles, in red ink on a large sheet of paper; I carry this in the pouch tied to my waist. I realize that there is no such thing as self-reliance. What looks like individual effort is actually made up of inputs from several sources. This gives me strength and connects me to things and people around.

Sosa is more representative of a bygone prosperity than the village of Pangu. A cobbled courtyard forms the centre of stone-walled, double-storeyed houses in the wealthy part of the village. Bunches of garlic, an important commercial produce of the area, hang outside solid wooden doors. Their dried sienna colour blends into the heavily carved unpainted wood; both take on a golden hue in the gentle light of the morning sun.

Rejuvenated by the tea break we start on the path winding through a valley, past hurtling rivulets, over which narrow planks of wood serve as bridges. Energy, beauty, power co-mingle and co-exist here. Their resonance reverberates somewhere deep within me. A tiny brick structure stands enigmatically in the middle of the strong current of a rivulet. An old man has just stopped his water mill after grinding some barley. Savouring nature, becoming a part of it, is a part of the yatra. Many of the group, propelled by ingrained urban habits, rush on to the next destination.

Man Singh tells me that most children here go to school and there is now a new college. People in the hills are becoming aware of issues like education, population and the need to preserve their environment. Those of his generation do not believe in having many children; he himself has two. He considers his young wife educated and himself unlettered. She has attended school till class two and is keen that their children are educated; she also helps them read. She works in the fields while he transports loads on mules. The yatras have given him a fillip, he has increased his stock of animals. The one I ride is a new acquisition. He intends to buy another mule near the border with Tibet.

After a good walk we reach Narayana Ashram. Built by the dedicated Narayana Swami in the 1930s, the ashram cultivates a rare variety of flowers in neatly maintained beds.

The size and the unusual colours of the dahlias surprises us. The beautifully maintained temple with a large hall is visited by all. Narayana Swami, originally from Karnataka, spent his life working for the uplift of the villagers in the area; he had been to Kailash several times. The ashram was built with the help of the villagers. It also serves as a haven for tired travellers. Gangotri Mataji, who is in charge, greets the group. I arrive almost an hour after the first lot of yatris. Since Mataji decided to deliver her lecture only after I reach, there is some irritation among the yatris who have had to wait. I am also irritated by their attitude because I do not want to rush through each walk. Strained feelings are temporarily soothed when Mataji begins to talk while hot tea and generous helpings of steaming halwa are served.

Located at a height of about 3,000 metres, the ashram is an apt reminder of the peculiar nature of our path. Often we found ourselves going up to 3,000 metres or more, only to come down to 800 metres and then up again. The elusive spiritual path also gives a sense of euphoria, only to plunge one back into depths of confusion when faced with a difficult situation in life. In these moments one realizes that there are just no short cuts to the discipline and practice required for self-development.

An easy descent through verdant surroundings brings us to Sirkha, a major village of the Dharchula tehsil, with a population of about 300 families. Brilliant shades of red and bright orange form interesting patterns on a large, paved courtyard. Though they look like red chillies from a distance, they are in fact different varieties of beans. As we pass through this courtyard we notice the colonial-style house of the village postmaster. With its green awnings and wrought-iron railings, the house stands out. I wonder if initially it housed an Englishman or an Indian.

On one side of the mountain, a kind of shed has been built over a swift mountain stream. Water is collected here to enable villagers to bathe and wash; it is a busy area. Women stand behind piles of clothes as children run around playfully.

A pair of eyes peer from a small window above the courtyard. In the courtyards of stone houses, too, women are busy at work. In the middle courtyard, an older woman works on her loom, one end wrapped around her waist and the other hooked on to a nail in the wall. This is the 'loin loom' popular in the eastern slopes of the Himalayas as well. The woman weaves a narrow strip of very hairy material. It will be joined with other strips to make a shawl for the severe winter. Rugs are woven on looms and stretched out on rectangular frames that stand up vertically. The weave is thick and designs are made to suit the taste of the village's nouveau riche. Older patterns with mellow colours and fine designs can only be seen on worn-out pieces on the backs of mules and ponies. Any desire to buy the rugs is soon dispelled by the high prices demanded. Bargaining, too, is an uneven exercise as the visitor is left to face all the villagers who gather together on one side. Even the weaver is left with little choice to make her own deal.

At the other end of the courtyard is a billy goat with long curved horns and shaggy hair. These muscular goats have been and still are used for carrying cargo up to 25 kilograms each. Their long hair makes the extraordinarily warm Tibetan wool.

Looking up, we spy a woman in the far reaches of the mountain. Her high perch sends a dizzying tingle down my spine. Firm-footed as a goat, she collects fodder, makes a huge bundle, and sends it spiralling down the slope. Men sit on roof-tops, smoking. Our guide Lalit Mohan tells us that it is the women who do most of the work. Even *chakti*, the sweet fermented drink made from locally grown millet, is brewed by women. This is much favoured by the men in uniform who spend long periods in these lonely regions without other means of entertainment. The ponywallahs spend happy evenings in this camp. Sirkha is looked upon as the most comfortable camp, with better toilet and water facilities.

Confronting our Individualities

(In the first section of the *Devi Mahatmyam* two demons, Madhu and Kaitabha, appear from the ear wax of a sleeping Vishnu. The two threaten Brahma who represents creative intelligence. For Brahma to be functional it is important for Vishnu to be awake. And Vishnu wakes up when Shakti, in the form of ignorance or sleep, resolves to leave him).

This great cosmic consciousness, Vishnu, is himself enveloped as it were in Maya, in sleep. While Vishnu is sleeping, Brahma the Creator has emerged and is being threatened by the demons. A sleeping person cannot wake himself up. He needs somebody or something else, an alarm clock or a splash of cold water. What a peculiar fate that a sleeping person cannot wake himself up, but sleep has to leave him. Sleep, that extremely intangible nothing, has such power that it can make a genius, a Nobel prize winner, appear stupid. However intelligent and powerful a man may be, he cannot wake himself up, but sleep has to decide to leave him.

Swami Venkatesananda
The Cosmic Dance

Sirkha proves to be a turning point for me. My friend, the Liaison Officer of an earlier group, had forewarned me about divisions in the group which would influence the general mindset of the yatris. Some who have been on this yatra before are restless to start a parallel leadership. My late arrival at the Narayana Ashram has become a tacit reason for doing so. At the usual nightly briefing I am told that the youngsters would like to move faster. According to our guides, our group has an unusually large number of elderly people, so moving together is important. But my voice is drowned in a din of disconnected noise; firmness will be required if the group is to hold together.

I feel a sense of betrayal at the turn of events. Is this all that this great venture means to us? Is it only trivialities that are going to engage our attention? Is it impossible for us to perform our individual yatras while being considerate to the needs of the group as a whole?

The sense of disquiet does not leave me as I lie down to sleep. I notice a huge rat and it brings up the mundane dread of contaminated food bags. I try to meditate. The six other occupants of the room are in the oblivion of sleep. Suddenly, I sense the rat climbing on to my shoulder – I almost jump up with a scream.

I must finally have dozed off, for I suddenly come awake later, in the stillness of the night. I was dreaming, walking through green fields. Ahead is a watermill with a thatched roof, water gushing under it. When I reach it I come to a bifurcation in the path. Unsure of the direction to take, the voice of an old man from inside the mill tells me to take the path that leads to Dev Darshan. I cannot see the man but his voice rings clear and loud. However, just before he can point out the path, I come awake. A reminder that I must not forget my own yatra in the melee of trivia. I still do not know the direction that will lead me to Dev Darshan or what the words mean in this context!

Dawn begins to gently cut through the darkness when I wake up again. I go out to breathe in the fresh morning air and shake myself free of last night's gloom. The mountain shadows are faint and long, the air calm. There is a stillness about the mountain silhouettes even as they reach out upward. John Snelling has written that it is 'the capacity of mountains to link earth and heavens, the twin spheres of men and gods, [that] serves to make their summits ideal situations for altars, shrines and temples.' He writes of the Chinese who have traditionally displayed a high degree of sensitivity to natural phenomena and their deeper qualities. In the *I Ching*, the Chinese *Book of Changes*, the hexagram associated with the mountain is *Ken* or *Keeping Still*. Snelling explains:

> The symbolism of *Ken* is full of intimations of meditation. It is a state of strong immovability; of perfect balance . . . a state in which all motion hangs suspended, not in death or inertia but in that great stillness that is the origin and resolution of all things. Like a great meditating sage a mountain sits with solidity upon the surface of the earth, quietly accumulating massive protean energies.[1]

As I stand contemplating the pre-dawn shadows, Soman approaches mumbling about a pain in the stomach. The apprehension brought on by the yatra makes this young man nervous. A little later Naresh appears saying he has a severe pain in the knee. He is deeply dejected at the thought that he may have to abandon this. long-yearned-for journey, just as it was becoming interesting. I persuade him to hire a pony and avoid strain.

There was a light drizzle in the pre-dawn hours, but rain gives way in the morning to let us pass. It is as if a silent pact recognizes our mutual needs and allows a fair sharing of time and space. The movement out of the camp, however, is disorderly. Some amble out early while others loll around; a tense, almost forced quiet pervades. I am perplexed and disturbed but decide not to react. I try to remember the teachings of the Masters: 'Actions must not arise from a conditioned perception of the immediate situation. Real action is not a reaction.' Waiting has its advantage as it brings clarity to the mind.

Naresh makes his way limping, trying to avoid riding. The problems are more on account of nervousness. A recognition is already beginning to emerge that no one can move alone as an individual unit. Fortunately, the majority of the yatris are performing well, largely untroubled by physical inconvenience.

Our passage out of the village is through a long, muddy descent, which the rain has made slippery. In the neighbouring Simkhola village, we see children in white and blue uniforms walking to their school near Sirkha. Mountain streams cross our path; on both sides, there are oaks and tall deodars. 'This is the kerosene of the mountains,' quips Man Singh, referring to their use as fuel. The denudation of the forest here is a little less than in the lower reaches. There is a strict watch on the felling of trees. Trees that are not of great commercial use are of value to the locals; their leaves are used to line the floors of cowsheds. In winter they keep the animals warm and make cleaning easier.

The walk today is long. For me it is a day of rumination and of maintaining harmony and unity in the group. The air is cool, and had it not been for the heavy tree cover, the sun would have beaten us down. Crossing Rungling Top at more than 3000 metres, we make a weary descent through uneven rocks. A number of mule trains of the handsome and large Australian variety walk smartly past us; they carry supplies for the jawans located in remote places. We still move westwards, away from the river that guides our path. The rocky configuration does not allow us to be near its edge.

Galla Ghat is a beautiful camp. Situated above and near a river gorge, it is surrounded by terraced fields growing beans and some quick-ripening grains that are harvested before the frost sets in. The little roadside shops stock soap, tea, matches and some stale-looking biscuits. There is enough *Chakti* to keep the local men occupied.

Tomorrow a treacherous part of the journey is to be manoeuvred. If it rains, it will make the journey all the more difficult and challenging. In any case, the older people may need help from the younger ones. An inner compulsion makes me call a meeting at teatime instead of the after-dinner hour. The message that yatras are for inner development and not just for proving one's physical prowess must somehow be communicated. Swami Krishnananda has said:

> The difference between the spiritual march and your march along the road or a highway is this: that while in you march on a roadway, you walk alone and nobody need accompany you, nothing need be connected with you, and you can have a free walk independently; in the spiritual march, it is not such an isolated march, you carry with you everything that is connected with you.[2]

The reference here is to the connection of the individual to his or her own emotions, past as well as present. It also refers to the connection of the individual to the whole, the cosmos

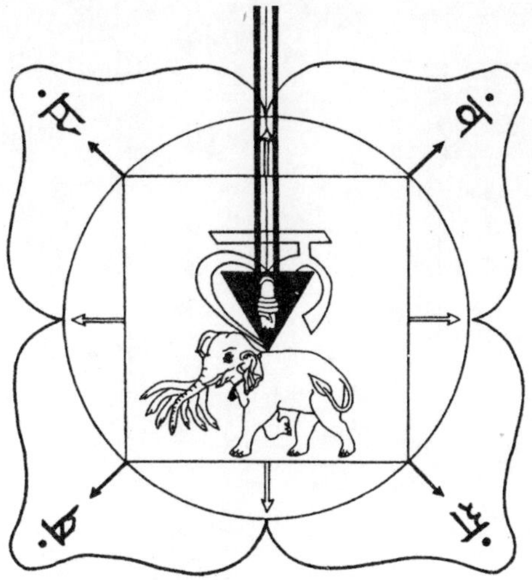

Muladhara Chakra.

and its constituent elements. The yatra is a reminder of that integral co-existence.

At this stage it is enough for us to recognize that the things connected with us are our co-travellers. We have to psychologically adjust to their needs and move in harmony. Then alone will the yatra be of any consequence. Then alone will it be enjoyable. Our teatime meeting has the desired impact. There is a perceptible lifting of the pall of divisiveness. Tripathiji suggests that no one should miss the evening *satsang*, which should be made a daily routine. A new life is breathed into the group. We have faced our overmuch engagement with our own separate individualities. An expansion out of our limited selves is necessary to bring meaning to our endeavour.

I feel that here we have come face-to-face with the first challenge the need to rise above the mundane and the trivial – the first stage where the most basic mental tranformation could take place.

Through the Locks of Shiva

> The matted locks of Shiva spread out as matter – as roots and rocks and interminable forests extending up to the ends of the four directions. The current of pranic energy remains concealed in them until released by the grace of Shiva himself or as a result of *tapas* invoked by humans.

It is Ganesh Chaturthi, and the people from Mumbai chant an invocation to *Ganapati Bappa* in Marathi. Ganesh or Ganapati, the son of Shiva and Parvati, the god who is the remover of obstacles, is a favoured deity in Maharashtra. The fast tempo of the chant is accompanied by rhythmic clapping; this becomes a part of our morning prayers which have so far consisted of *shlokas* in praise of Shiva. The verses and rhythms replaying in our heads will remind us of the journey long after we return. Verses and mantras chanted in crisp, fast-moving rhythm or a slow and reverberating one, touch some basic chords in our bodies and leave a deep impression. The sonic vibrations set into motion in this natural environment make a deep impact on our mental and physical systems.

Today, everyone is ready at five-thirty without demur. Most yatris are out five minutes before schedule, and the baggage is handed over to the contractor. Kiran hangs around again, her horseman is not there. This time I manage to persuade her to start moving ahead of him. The oldest in the group, Bhairavi also complains about her ponywallah: 'The man is too old, his horse too is old.' Her inappropriate high-heeled sandals slip and make her tumble on the stretches where even mules find it difficult to tread firmly. Some of us spent months preparing ourselves, but it is clear that Bhairavi left home without a thought to what might be required.

Durga takes it upon herself to help the older woman. A tacit but clear sense of sisterhood marks her attitude. As a member of a mountaineering club in Kolkata, she has developed a sporting and adventurous spirit. In moments when I am alienated by the group because of a particular decision, I hear Durga's supportive voice rising above the others. Sometimes, she reads aloud from her book to enlighten us about the historical and religious background of our camps. Her peculiar mixture of Bengali, Hindi and English becomes a charming source of diversion. Dull moments are lightened by her particular brand of humour. She tends to see the funny side of serious and irritating incidents. I develop an affection for her open and uninhibited nature.

The departure from Galla takes place before dawn. Finally, Bhairavi's old horseman turns up. Perched on her horse, feet floating in my large spare shoes, she moves on. We have been told that this is the most difficult part of the trek. The sheer drop and the rough uneven steps seem formidable.

A short walk brings us to the little temple at the head of the steep descent. The track consists of some six kilometres of step-like rocks, most of them two or three feet high. Known locally as *Bindakoti ki chaddhai*, after the village which stands at its head, this is preferably traversed before the sun becomes too hot. There are no streams along this stretch, an anomaly, since the area receives a good amount of rainfall. All that the rain does is to make the path treacherous. One slip here could take one down at least 300 metres. An enterprising Bhotia has set up a small tent on a ledge with space enough for two. He sells mountain cucumbers as large as gourds. Water carried in buckets from Jipti, a kilometre away, is used to make tea. On the way back, when these mammoth steps will have to be climbed up, this little kiosk will provide much relief to parched throats. Porters take a break here to feed on juicy slices of cucumber.

We descend 1,000 metres or more before the Kali meets us again. Lalit Mohan, our guide, has evolved his own method of covering these distances. He keeps up a continuous chatter about the area, the people and anecdotes about earlier groups of yatris. The area has developed significantly since the yatras officially began in 1981. Before that, the local people had no idea of the ways of city dwellers (as though that were something of a qualification). Now they have learnt much, and the yatras have revived business. The older people who live here move down to Dharchula and its vicinity when winter approaches. In fact, they descend with the last group of yatris.

Helped by ponywallahs and some of the younger yatris, Bhairavi makes her descent safely. The untidy-looking jolly couple also go down safely.

I overhear Rudra holding forth on a *stotra* dedicated to Ganesh. He has found a ready listener in Mishra, a younger wireless operator. Rudra's Hindi is poor and Mishra's English limited, yet Rudra spares no effort to make his message clear and to teach the willing captive. His reverence for the subject demands that the listener absorb its full meaning.

'What is Gaja?'

'Elephant.'

'Anana?'

'Face.'

'Gajanan?'

'Elephant-faced.'

And so the discourse progresses, going into the various aspects of the god. Mishra fluently recites the thirty-two names of Durga Devi.

Rudra and Sita Ram, a PAC guard, do not walk together. Both need listeners, so Sita Ram slips alongside me. His memory and capacity for narrating stories replete with homilies is unlimited. During flat or downward stretches, he prattles continuously. During ascents the heavy task of breathing demands full concentration and he is compelled to give his vocal cords a rest. He is generally asked to start out as the front guard, with the first lot of yatris. We know he will slowly fall back eventually bringing up the rear. Sita Ram has voluntarily asked for this assignment, which others avoid or refuse due to the hardship involved. His philosophical inclination demands that he go through the varied aspects of nature for the development of his mind. Never mind if he cannot reach Kailash, at least he would have savoured the beauty of *prakriti*, nature. He is aware of our indulgent attitude towards him as he regales us with anecdotes from the *Ramayana* and other texts in his eastern Bihari style of singing. The story of Sita's abduction by Ravana is narrated with gusto, as also the incarnations of Vishnu from *satya* through *treta* to *dvapara* yuga.

The young trekkers prefer lighter film songs. Sita Ram does not disappoint them: he has a number of amusing Bhojpuri songs about secret meetings between lovers. At campsites, his voice can be heard above that of other PAC constables as they sit around for 'instruction' from him.

Besides revealing the hidden facets of each personality, the yatra reminds us to respect everything, even things that earlier seemed useless. The knee caps provided long ago by Lakshmi, my friend in Australia, come in handy now. The vigorous testing of joints on the steep steps near the eastern gate of Lodhi Gardens in New Delhi has proved useful. The trek has made me aware of tendons and ligaments that I was not aware of before.

We reach Lakhanpur at nine in the morning, having traversed a difficult section of the yatra. At a place where the river spreads out delta-like, there are three tea shops under a giant promontory. *Parathas* are eagerly unpacked and fresh ones ordered together with *chai.*

Lakhanpur is a distortion of the Bhotia-Tibetan word *Lakhar Phu,* or large cave. There is a subtle cultural gradation in the Bhotias from Dharchula to Lipu Pass, where we cross over into the Tibetan desert. All belong to the Ranga Samaj and represent different shades of ethnicity even as the groups merge into one other. Those in the upper reaches are more akin to Tibetans while lower down they have assimilated with the plains people. They also intermarry across the border with Nepalis.

Lakhar Phu is 2,400 metres above sea level. The descent has brought us level with the river. The path now winds under narrow rock promontories, sometimes we have to bend and go across. Rapid waterfalls rush down from mountain crags as though the Ganga in her turbulent descent from heaven had decided to carry down whatever came in her way. Ganga literally means the flowing channel; it refers to an irresistible flow of the great river of life whose essential nature is movement. It is the flow of energy between heaven and earth, between the *devas* and material manifestations.[1] Hence its purifying ability. As we plough through the path that appears like the matted locks of Shiva, the river of life present in all the nooks and crevices, invigorates and strengthens the effort.

One of the falls is appropriately called *Chhaata,* as water here gushes down the concave hood of an umbrella-shaped rock. We crouch and try to go across quickly, holding umbrellas; I try to save the small recorder in my waist belt. Partly soaked, I dry out quickly in the crisp, warm air.

In places the rocks have been cut to make space for pilgrim traffic. The Public Works Department (PWD) has hired local wage labour on watch, to look out for landslides and immediately make the road passable for this time-bound yatra. Even so, an earlier group had to abandon the onward journey. The employed men feel their job is significant, as they are helping the yatris through. On our right, a small wooden bridge across the river leads into Nepal. It is never difficult to cross over from one side to the other, the villagers own land on both sides.

We have to now tackle what looks like a 70-degree gradient. The path winds straight up alongside a multi-fanged fall that licks the granite slopes with electric energy. The light mists floating over valleys and mountains and scant human habitation make us feel we are walking on ethereal ground. Silence and tranquility are palpably intermingled with the ferocity and energy of the elements. The destructiveness of nature together with her protective and preserving aspect, inspire awe – what looked frightening a moment ago seems sacerdotal the next. A slight shift in the angle changes one vision into another.

We reach Malpa by one o'clock, and soon spread our wet clothes out on the hot, dry rocks. Resting directly on the boulders of the Kali, Malpa is a small bowl in the midst of a mountainous synod. Lalit Mohan had told us earlier that this is the most boring camp. Trapped between mountains, the village probably has only two houses.

The turbulence of the Kali resonates like the rage of Shiva in his dance of destruction. For jaded urbanites, it is like being in the womb of the earth, in direct contact with her primal energy. The unceasing roar of the river drowns most other sounds. Later in the evening, even the *satsang* becomes audible only when local staff together with the Indo-Tibetan Border Police and the medical personnel based here join us. They bring cymbals and *jhanj* to enliven the singing.

Our baggage is yet to come; Bhairavi paces in and out restlessly. I imagine she requires something urgently. When the baggage arrives she pulls in her two small bags, places them beside her, and lies down to rest.

The young girl complains about losing a sheet: 'I packed it this morning and now it is not in the bag. And they say no one steals here!' A quarter of an hour later, rummaging through her bags, she finds it. The old man next only to Bhairavi in age, whimpers, 'See how they have dumped my things in the rain.' Nerves are jangled, and they affect responses. Deepa insists that the contractor is not doing his job properly. Even in this remote part of the world it is our own selves that we confront: 'Is there no electricity here?'; 'The food here is awful.' It is as though the fears and anxieties regarding the attainment of the goal have themselves become obstacles in achieving it.

Malpa is more sparsely equipped than other camps; plastic bags are not available for packing our breakfast the following morning. We must eat before we leave. This does not really pose a problem because the next camp can be comfortably reached even if we start by 8 a.m. Having become used to an early schedule, we start by seven in the morning. The route is easy, without any sharp drops or ascents. Deodars now give way to *chir*. Terraced fields along the way are carpeted with little pink flowers which yield small-grained seeds called *phaphar*. In the plains, these seeds are ground into flour and used during the days of fasting before Dussehra. During the nine days of *Navratri* puja, *phaphar* flour forms a substitute for the disallowed regular cereals. The flowers that enliven the landscape are harvested before the frost sets in.

There are other flowers too – rhododendrons, dandelions and columbines. At 9.30 we stop at Lamare for tea. KMVN has extended a loan to the owner for setting up the shop. The policy of giving out loans is expected to encourage the setting up of more shops for the benefit of yatris. The owner of this one has a small field where she grows maize and vegetables together with cucumbers and gourds. The surplus is sold to visitors.

The air is crisp and riding on the back of Samli is joyful as it allows me to give unalloyed attention to the landscape. A little later a couple of PWD men join us in the walk to Buddhi. They talk about their stay in the area and are happy for this leisurely diversion. We reach at eleven, and the entrance to the Buddhi camp is lined with flower beds. It is a guesthouse meant for the local PWD officials. There is a concrete structure for the kitchen and below it another building for the officials. We use its verandah for our daily medical check-up. Nearby is a relatively well-stocked shop. We buy biscuits and other provisions to celebrate Sandeep's birthday today. I feel doubly enthusiastic because it is also my son Vikram's birthday.

Buddhi is the last postal station. From the next camp on, our letters will be carried by the PAC men who go down from time to time. Closer to higher ranges the mountains look even more enticing now. On one side of the camp, we can see the winding path we have traversed and a new road which is being built. On the other side, the mountains are ranged formidably.

Water here is plentiful and the sun bright. That and our early arrival provides us the opportunity to wash and dry our clothes. Long treks over the next few days will provide no occasion for such luxuries. Soon the rocks around our camp are covered with the many shapes, sizes and colours of our clothes. The sun is heady, the atmosphere wonderfully relaxed. Some yatris lounge around in the small verandah, others use the occasion to catch up on sleep. As we sit on the boundary wall relishing the sun, we notice the tall dark mountain ahead which we are to negotiate tomorrow. A number of ranges have to be crossed over to reach the plateau that rests in serene tranquility beyond the dense vegetation and shrubbery. One of the locals brings us some crisp and juicy mountain apples. The *satsang* at night is festive. The biscuits and candies obtained from the shop make for sumptuous prasad.

Shakti in the Mountains

> I stretch the bow of Shiva for the protection of those who take refuge in me. I pervade the earth and sky as their innermost being.
>
> Rig Vedic *Devi Suktam*

The trek begins at 6.30 after breakfast. We are faced with a steep ascent known as *Chiyalik ki Chaddhai.* This three-kilometre climb, literally, takes our breath away, as though every step forward is on near vertical ground. Below us is a sheer drop of 2000 feet. The camp looks like a speck, and the winding path is etched out like a line drawn on a map. After some time I succumb to Man Singh's suggestion and get on to Samli's back. I must hold on to the animal and bend forward so as not to slide off her back. As we go deeper into the heart of the Himalaya, we get an exhilarating feeling of being in contact with the power of nature at its purest. The mind feels liberated as it stretches to mingle with the unimaginable peace and serenity around. Riding on these tortuous paths is becoming a source of joy. The narrow Chiyalik Pass stands at the head of this ascent and is barely three feet wide. The first signs of cultural diversity are visible here. An arch connects the two sides of the pass. Stretched across it is a string from which hang innumerable prayer flags or votive offerings. We see many more of these as we proceed. Another range is crossed as we move through the pass.

Immediately, we are met with a pleasant surprise, a high-altitude meadow, also called a bugiyal. A uniformed man greets and invites us into the ITBP camp situated atop the pass. We are served hot coffee and fried potatoes. Between mouthfuls, Sandeep jocularly remarks that if his food processing plant churned out potato chips like these he would soon go out of business.

Set in the shadow of the Kanchenjunga ranges, the camp has the aura of a meditation retreat. Winter here must be severe and only those sound in mind and body could remain whole in such utter solitude. Across the path from the camp is the ancient Vyas Mandir, and the ITBP has built a new structure beside it. Sage Vyas is said to have spent many years in these parts; he is known for his voluminous work which comprises *the Brahma Sutras*, *Mahabharata,* an exposition on the *Vedas*, and *Srimad Bhagvatam.* Perhaps he composed much of his work on *bhojpatras*, made from the bark of bhoj trees that grow in these high altitudes. I am given some as a sample by one of our PAC guards. Light brown in colour with a smooth texture, their resemblance to fine hand-made paper is remarkable.

The bugiyal is ablaze with colour. Rare wild flowers grow in abundance here. It is easy to see why the sages of yore scaled these heights to engage their minds with sublime thoughts. The rarified atmosphere induces lightness in the mind and somehow removes the burden of memory, a baggage that muddies thought.

A number of medicinal herbs grow here. The forest is suffused with a sweet smell. Over the past few days, I have been attracted by the unusual fragrance of the cooking fire lit by the porters. The reason for it becomes clear now. The wood used by them belongs to the trees and shrubs that have special qualities. It brings to mind an episode in *Valmiki Ramayana*: Ram and Lakshman fall unconscious due to the special weapon used by Indrajit. Most of Ram's army is grounded, as it is heavily wounded. Then Jambavan, one of the tribal leaders, asks Hanuman to bring a special herb. From the southern tip of India, Hanuman travels a distance of one thousand *yojanas*, crosses the golden Rishabha Parvat, from which the peak of Kailash can be seen. He then crosses Malayachal Parvat, high like Meru, to come to Aushadhi Parvat which glows, as it were, with medicinal plants. Just the smell of the herbs brought by Hanuman heals the wounds of the warriors and rejuvenates them for further fighting.[1]

The side of the mountain along the Mana Pass has been requisitioned by an Ayurvedic firm to collect medicinal herbs. On the side where we are, herbs are fewer and more difficult to collect but the ponywallas and Bhagwan Singh of the PAC know where the valuable *pama* grass (from which *gokul dhoop* is made for ritual worship) can be obtained. This is invaluable in the performance of *havans*, propitiatory rites and rituals. Steep mountainsides have to be scanned to find the real medicinal grasses. Later, on the way back from Tibet, we are given some of these rare herbs, collected by the PAC constables.

Fortified by the tea, we resume our journey. The walk continues through the beautiful meadow; the level walk is a welcome change after the steep climb. We have again moved west of the river. The sight of the Annapurna peaks touched by the gold of the morning sun is thrilling. The peak in the foreground looks like a smooth marble dome, polished to perfection. It evokes an ecstatic, prayerful mood. The serene contours of this golden dome remain behind us throughout the day. So mesmerizing are they that I cannot stop turning around to gaze at them.

We can spot small whitewashed structures with pinnacled roofs from which flags sway gaily, on top of most of the low-lying hills. These are temples dedicated to Devi or Shakti. In the hills it is mostly the goddess, the creative aspect of Shiva that is worshipped. The temples are a tribute to the life-giving force of nature as well as a recognition of its invincible might before which humans are rendered powerless.

The village of Garbyang is visible in the valley some distance below. Before we reach it, Tripathiji takes me to a little shrine by the path, near his ponywallah's home. The ponywallah's son comes up panting, with a flask full of hot tea, made from pure cow's milk, just as we arrive. He touches his father's feet in respectful greeting before pouring out the tea for us. Soon after, Tripathiji disappears into the village with his ponywallah while I carry on with Man Singh. A majority of the others have mostly gone ahead, only one or two trail behind.

At nine, we approach Garbyang. Most of the buildings here look prosperous, with carved pillars and ornate doorways, far richer than the ones we have passed by. But an extraordinary piece of information awaits us here: none of these structures have stable foundations! The whole mountainside has moved down and the buildings have moved with it. The houses, though apparently intact, are literally on shaky ground. They remain uninhabited as most of the villagers have moved to Palang. It is an eerie feeling to encounter houses standing on shifting clay with walls that could collapse at any time. An ITBP building has moved all the way down to the river level, from its original position higher up on the mountain. This is one of the structures in which there is still some activity. The ghost village attracts a handful of people on the lookout for making money during the yatra season. They set up tea shops in a couple of vacant houses and even provide overnight accommodation for some stray souls. With the last of the yatra groups, these villagers also move down.

Garbyang was the last important town on the Indian side during the heydays of Indo-Tibetan trade. Until the fragile mountain made habitation impossible, Garbyang was a major stopover for those crossing into Tibet. It was home to some of the wealthiest Bhotias and a trading centre. Wool and rock salt were traded for the grains grown in these valleys. It was also known for dacoits and ferocious dogs. Today it looks like a royal village deserted long ago for more stable, even if stark surroundings, further up.

The river span here is extremely narrow. According to myth, the ruling deity of Garbyang blocked the way when Kali, in the form of a river, wanted to pass through. Kali is worshipped as the goddess who devours evil. When Kali prayed, the deity agreed to provide only a narrow passage but not without incurring a curse from the goddess. So the river flows through a narrow passage here, but the earth of Garbyang remains friable and continues to slide downwards. In this great flux, Garbyang may go out of existence but Kali will continue its tumultuous descent downward.

The conglomerate of rubble, sand and stones on which Garbyang is located sedimented here more than a 100 thousand years ago, but the rocks underneath it are about 60 million years old. When the tectonic crunching of the continental plates took place, the oceanic bed of the Tethyan Sea was raised to expose its bed of rocks and sand to the winds and the sun. In time, a rock face fell and dammed the Kali river. This resulted in the formation of a large lake in which sediments consisting of sand, loam and other materials from the upper region were deposited. Slowly, Kali again carved out a path for herself. But the water of the river continues to seep through the soft loam and sand which is further broken down by heavy cloudbursts that characterize the region. The result is the continuous shifting of the mountainside. A number of fossilized sea creatures can be found in the rocks here, right up to the Kailash-Manasarovar region.[2]

Water from the mountain springs here breaks up and hems the slopes in the form of delicate waterfalls. This is another form taken by Shakti, the inherent and ceaseless striving of the Supreme to manifest Itself. Being an aspect of the eternal and the limitless, its potential for manifestation is also infinite. The only thing that remains constant is Shakti, the potential that inheres the forms.

Immediately after Garbyang, we pass a stretch of extremely slippery soil trodden already by men of the PWD or the ITBP. Their store of winter rations has to pass through this place before the snows make it impossible. We are lucky not to have any rain, and be able to go through without risking life and limb. The narrow path makes it necessary to walk singly and carefully.

The journey to Gunji is long, but it continues to provide vistas of all aspects of nature. The destructive and the creative are again palpably visible here. Shrubs of *chuk*, an extremely sour lemon-like fruit used mainly for chutneys and pickles (Swami Pranavananda mentions its presence even in the upper reaches of Tibet), and some bright red translucent berries which surrender themselves to the piercing rays of the sun, line both sides of the path. We walk through the vast fields of yellow and cornflower-blue blossoms; the golden Annapurna peaks form a dramatic backdrop to the fields. It is difficult to believe that this exuberance is totally unmediated by human effort. Tired limbs are forgotten as the mind mingles with the surroundings. It is no surprise that the area is called *Deva Bhumi*, Land of the Gods.

There are small patches of bright red crops encircled by barbed wire. This fencing accentuates the bounteousness of nature which throws itself open to one and all. The colours belong to the ripening grains of *phaphar* and *palthi*, the staple of the sparse local population, and soon to be harvested. This is the only crop cultivated in the whole year.

We walk through stretches displaying fantastic alluvial movements. Huge chunks of porous rock that have been dislodged and vast tracts of scree laid bare by the ceaseless motion of wind and waters surround us. In the midst of such movement it is not a wonder that every earthly projection is dedicated to Devi, the elusive Maya of the Unchanging One, the mobile aspect of the static. Some temples are also dedicated to Shiva, the Being from which She cannot be separated, to whom She gives form but without whom She could not exist. The Divine Androgyny in its elemental form finds expression in natural phenomena here.

We move west while the course of the Kali continues in a southwardly direction, undeterred by insurmountable boulders. It makes a stupendous gorge but we cannot follow it. The river points the direction, but the path we choose is determined by our limitations. Inner contours arise and fade till only those that are relevant to the goal emerge more clearly. Priorities fall into a different context in this vast impersonal expanse and display of energy.

The camp at Gunji becomes visible. The mountainous path has a chimera-like quality, making the destination appear just a stone's throw away, when the actual path has to wind through a valley and around another mountain. Even so, the sight is heartening and gives hope to our tired limbs. We walk through the village of Nepulchu, a cluster of solidly constructed double-storeyed houses made of stone. A new stone building under construction is the primary school. The children now have the facility of education even during the brief summer period which they may spend here with their parents or grandparents. They will continue their studies when they move down to Dharchula in the winter. Neat rows of blazing red *phaphar* outline the approach to the village. We cross a wooden bridge over a glacial stream arising in Chhota Kailash, a mountain located on the Indian side. Another steep climb, and then the village of Gunji.

A deep sound of drums resonates through the village. It originates from an inner courtyard in the heart of the village. Man Singh and I enter it through a stone arch to find a group of drummers seated behind huge kettledrums and large cymbals. This is the day of the yearly homage to Dhami, the village deity which protects it from evil spirits; the pole that bears prayer flags is replaced on this day with great festivity. The choice and the changing of the pole is a solemn ritual. A flawless cedar with a tall, sturdy trunk is selected and carried here by a group of able-bodied villagers. New prayer flags are strung on it in accompaniment to prayers and rhythmic music. No work is done for three days, and there is much drinking of *chakti* while appeasing the deity. As I flourish my recorder to hold their sounds, the play becomes more enthusiastic. They tell me to wait till they are ready for yet another rhythm. One group carrying huge cymbals materializes from an adjoining room. Much amusement is caused when I take a photograph.

Behind the houses lining the courtyard there is a large black rock, about five feet high and four feet in diameter. It is said that this was brought here by a single person, all by himself, from the mountainside. So it has been installed here, to be worshipped. There are myriads of prayer flags strung around it. The tall deodars, or *devadaru,* the wood of the gods, brings to mind the story of Shiva and Vishnu. The two decided to test the rishis and sages who were performing austerities in the *devadaru vana.* They paired up together, one as a naked ascetic and the other as a beautiful woman. The woman's beauty attracted all the young male children of the rishis and the females could not keep away from the radiant ascetic. Annoyed by this, the rishis attacked the pair. Vishnu, the woman, fled while Shiva the ascetic held on. A number of things were hurled at him; even a demon-like elephant which was slain by him. The skin of the elephant was used by Shiva to cover his body. Since then, the trees and the land are seen as the playground of the gods.

Surprisingly, Gunji appears more developed than we expected. It is the most heavily populated village after Sirkha. The usual double-storeyed houses line the narrow lanes on both sides. The upper floors of the houses are reached by an ingenious device, the like of which we had first seen at Didihat: a solid tree trunk with steps cut into it, placed in a near vertical position and used by the locals with agility. Heavy carved doors adorn the houses. Outside some homes women who could pass off as Tibetans, sit at square-framed looms weaving carpets and woollen shawls.

A small room on the western side of the village has been turned into a dispensary run by a young boy during the non-yatra season. Despite a limp, he goes up the ladder easily to deposit some *pama* grass brought to him by friends from the mountains. I wonder how patients actually make their way up this contraption. The medical assistant, Varma, who has come all the way from Beri Nag in eastern Pithoragarh, stays only for the yatra period. After that the medical work falls back to the boy. A number of people flock to the medical assistant with minor and major complaints. When asked to come to the dispensary, near the ITBP camp where we are lodged, they say they have no time. Well aware of this trait of the villagers, Varma carries some common medicines and an injection syringe. He boils the syringe wherever possible and administers medicine on the move. The villagers look upon him as a god. Varma has been here for a few months, also attending to groups that have gone before us. He finds the villagers extremely hard-working. Whenever they have a free moment from the fields, the women work on their looms. There is a lot of variety in the weaves, and a number of new designs are woven. The Chinese influence, discernible in the dragon shape, is seen only occasionally; its execution is more difficult and time consuming. Many of the borders are in the Tibetan swastika style. The women are clever salespersons.

The houses are meticulously clean. We visit the home of a prosperous widow who trades in carpets and looks after her fields. Through a heavy-vaulted door we go up a flight of freshly plastered mud steps. They are so clean that I feel inclined to take off my filthy shoes but we are asked in as we are. The room is also neatly plastered with clean mud. A small window to the north opens out to a beautiful view of the mountains. This is an architectural feature we find in most Tibetan buildings. In the centre of the room is a square-shaped raised platform plastered with mud; it serves as a table for visitors. The hostess specially sends for a packet of black tea and some biscuits, the only possible snack available in these regions. Behind the spacious room is the kitchen – large, with a fireplace in the centre where wood is used for cooking. The walls and roof are covered with soot from the wood smoke. There is warmth and welcome in the atmosphere.

Further to the west of the village is a narrow path lined with *chir* and deodar trees leading to a Kali temple. This path leads to Chhota Kailash, the Indian counterpart of the Tibetan Kailash. A new, organized yatra to Chhota Kailash has been started by KMVN. It takes 17 days and does not entail a *parikrama* because Chhota Kailash does not stand alone by itself, as Kailash in Tibet does. Completed within India, the shorter yatra does not call for lengthy visa processes and other permissions. A group of yatris for this pilgrimage is expected to arrive in about two days.

About two kilometres from the village, the Kali temple stands hidden among the pines. If one did not know it existed, one could easily pass it by. There are some offerings of flags and billy-goat horns just outside the quaint-looking structure. There is no one inside, so it is possible to pray in solitude.

Our camp is more than a kilometre of strenuous walking from the village. The altitude, about 3,700 metres, has made this walk more difficult than it may otherwise have been. As usual the camp is set in a bowl in the mountains with the Api peaks forming the backdrop. But this camp is much more open. The region around appears devastated by floods. Huge spaces where water must once have flowed, now display large quantities of mountain effluent over pebbles and fine sand. There are signs of erosion and natural denudation all around.

Dr Pandey, who has accompanied us all through, is relieved of his duties at this camp. The routine medical check will now be carried out by an ITBP doctor. Having heard of the unnecessary fuss made by ITBP doctors, there is renewed tension among the group. Will this be the last camp for some of us? We know about Mrs Tiwari from another group who was told in Gunji that she had a weak heart. All tests earlier had indicated sound health and she had proved to be among the good walkers. She had begged to be allowed to go up to Kalapani, the next stop. At Kalapani too, the doctor had pronounced her unfit and compelled her to return. Back in Delhi, the ITBP hospital had found her to be totally fit. Later the ITBP sent her an apology for the mistake they had made during the yatra.

We find the doctor to be a non-troublesome man from Andhra Pradesh who opted for a posting here without knowing what it entailed. Nothing in the mountains pleases him; the altitude and the cold bother him constantly. No one else speaks his language, so he survives on the Telugu magazines he subscribes to. A lonely soul, he is happy to discover the company of Rudra and Ganapathi who speak Telugu.

Gunji lies open to howling winds that blow at hundred kilometres and more per hour. The school building next to the camp is still roofless, the wind blowing the roof away a year ago. The number of students at the school has dwindled; the majority have gone to the plains to study. The surroundings depict a ravaged, solitary beauty; there is extreme water scarcity here. A large drum filled from time to time serves as the single source of water supply in the camp.

The ITBP commander whose headquarters are located here invites us to celebrate the foundation day of his battalion, installed ten years ago. One of the duties expressly given to this wing of the border police is to conduct the yatris safely up to the Lipu Lekh Pass. From here on, Sethuram, the commander, accompanies us; he is spiritually inclined and carries out his duties with grace and humility.

The night sky at Gunji is a starry dome. The haze of city pollution is by now a distant memory. Stars alone, even without the moon, create enough light for visibility outside. The surrounding mountains end in temple-like crests, some with multiple spires, as though inspired by a divine architect.

It has been a long and tiring day. The 17-kilometre walk and subsequent activities are followed by long consultations with the ITBP personnel, regarding the journey ahead. By the time we finish it is late. I come back into a shack in which six bodies heave with rhythmic regularity. Our group has begun to seem like a replication of the path in which the negatives and the positives, the lows and highs, surface to make up the whole. In the morning, the first rays of the sun arising from behind the ranges create a golden nimbus around them, making them look like sacred shrines.

The Trivial and the Miraculous

There is more that is wondrous in nature than the human mind can imagine.

I leave the camp with Man Singh in tow after everyone has gone. We go up a steep sandy climb and minutes later, I become aware of a momentary blackout. It feels as if the air has been squeezed out of my lungs; I gasp for breath, mouth open. It is so sudden. Maybe the result of the tedious journey yesterday combined with the lack of rest. My body feels drained of energy and the limbs lifeless. I do not want anyone to notice this, not even Man Singh who keeps Samli on the ready. It is too early for the altitude to show its effect especially when the others seem to be doing well. Of course, they too may be putting up a front. I drag on, keeping up the small talk with my companion.

Just above the camp is an old temple dedicated to Veda Vyasa whose actual name was Krishna Dvaipaayan. A large statue of him stands behind locked bars in a cave-like temple dug out high up in the rock that forms the mountain. Nearby is an enclosed pit where a pair of sacred white adders appear – only to certain blessed people, it is said. Some ITBP men claim that every time they have visited the temple, the couple has appeared. But when they are accompanied by others, the adders remain invisible. A number of empty cans used for offering milk to the *sarpa devatas* are scattered in and around the pit. Since their appearance is believed to be auspicious, we spend long minutes awaiting their emergence.

After an hour of walking we rest for a while. I swallow glucose and amino acids and chew on raisins and nuts. Maya, a niece who had trekked in the Rockies, had insisted I carry enough GORP: Good Old Raisins and Peanuts. Their effect is not immediately discernible, so I decide to ride. It is a marvel that I do not slip off because a heavy drowsiness overtakes me and I doze off many a time. I am aware of fording streams, of going down steep inclines when I am asked to sit leaning backward to keep the balance. I am aware of the Kali that rejoins us, of the woods around, and am grateful that we perform the journey before the sun becomes unbearable.

Just before Kalapani there is a small sign pointing down to a hot sulphur spring. Some of the youngsters are already enjoying a bath, down by the river where the hot spring meets it. I move on. Crossing a small wooden bridge we come to a beautiful gate leading to a temple built by the PAC, who have their headquarters here. Outside the gate a stone slab reads: *Deva Darshan, Lipu 16,800 feet.* I am stunned to read the words that I heard in my dream. Does it mean that I am to go past Lipu and reach my destination or am I going to end my journey here? My body feels drained of blood. To walk the few steps to the temple is a major task. Every step makes me gasp for breath. I sit down in the courtyard outside the temple. The temple has two sections, one dedicated to Durga and the other to Shiva, and both have exquisitely carved stone statues. I invoke the deities to give me the strength to fulfil the wish of a lifetime. It is also a matter of prestige because I undertook the responsibility despite many obstacles.

Kalapani is so named because it is said to be the source of the river Kali. Outside the temple there is a pond which receives water from the Kali, an insignifcant dribble here. According to myth, the water comes here from Badri Narayana through an underground channel. Badri Narayana is one of the four major centres of Vedic culture set up in the four cardinal directions of India by Adi Shankaracharya. It is said that the stream dries up completely the day the doors of the temple at Badri close for winter; the water flows again when the doors open at the beginning of summer. This is confirmed by those who stay here.

Kalapani is a busy camp. All the immigration formalities are carried out here, before we cross the Himalayan ranges to enter Tibet. Passports are checked and emigration stamps affixed by an official who works from a small tent. As we will be allowed to open only one small piece of baggage at Navidhang, the next camp, it is necessary to ensure that the required gear is kept accessible by every yatri. The rest of the baggage is to be carried directly to Lipu Pass by the contractor, without a night halt at Navidhang. The climatic conditions during the ascent to Lipu can be unpredictable. So I approach Sethuram and borrow a parka, dark glasses and gloves for those who lack them. The helpful and obliging Sethuram manages to put together the required articles. Light clothing and other articles not required in the higher reaches are left behind. Our Indian currency is also to be deposited here; we are strictly warned not to carry any into Tibet except for the amount to be paid at Lipu to the ponywallahs and porters. The rest is collected, sealed and deposited in a KMVN safe-deposit vault. At night, while going to bed, a doubt begins to lurk in my mind: will I get up in the morning? I take some of the homeopathic medicine given by a helpful friend. 'This will act as your lungs in the mountain,' he had quipped. Later, I learn that it is a good idea to take a tablet of Calmpose at night in these altitudes. A comfortable sleep becomes an antidote to the breathing difficulty.

For the first time I understand fully the miracle of waking up after a night's sleep. We take this daily miracle for granted and do not realize its wondrous joy. I wish to prolong the pleasure of this revelation but it is abruptly ended by a heated discussion between the contractor and some yatris. The contractor refuses to allow even one piece of baggage to be opened at Navidhang. All of a sudden he seems quite belligerent. We have already packed believing that one bag each would be made available there, before we cross Lipu. But he does not want his men to cook a meal at Navidhang as that would entail carrying wood as none is available there. After much cajoling and arguing, he agrees to carry a limited number of pieces separately and these will be given to us at Navidhang. He and I leave the camp together at eight o'clock.

Leaving the source of the Kali behind, we go along a small stream. ITBP jawans now accompany us instead of our PAC friends. The ITBP man who accompanies me is going up for the first time. He gets out of breath quickly and finds it difficult to keep pace with the sturdy Man Singh. The route now is rocky and scrubby. The mountains on both sides are bare of trees and seem eroded. Massive lanslides from times gone by are visible.

At Kalapani we saw the cave in which Sage Vyasa is said to have meditated and composed the *Srimad Bhagavatam.* Having finished his monumental work on the Vedas and the Upanishads, the sage was still not satisfied; he felt he had done nothing worthwhile. He then had an insight that he would not enjoy the satisfaction he was yearning for till he composed a devotional work dedicated to the Divine. The *Bhagavatham,* which he composed thereafter, is a work in praise of the Supreme and its avatars who sought to free the world of its suffering. Those who have been to the cave have said that there is enough room inside for several people to sit and sleep. The sage may have instructed disciples here. The inaccessible height of the cave is supposed to be a result of massive erosions. What was earlier at ground level is now perched high.

The route to Navidhang is easy, as we ascend 600 metres in about nine kilometres. Like some other camps, Navidhang is situated at the meeting point of two streams, the Tinker coming from Nepal in the east and another one coming down the Lipu. We will be walking alongside the latter in the early hours of the morning. The journey to Navidhang is completed in about two hours. The KMVN manager greets us saying that the fantastic Om Parvat is hidden behind the clouds but these may clear up soon. In the past few days, the sky was cloudless and clear. This is the first camp where we have to sleep in tents. The excitement of coming almost to the end of the journey on the Indian side and of crossing into Tibet by the morning has gripped us all.

The ITBP have dug out a small temple dedicated to the Devi in a rock on the south side of the camp. No one wants to go inside their tents. We sit with our backs to the little temple and look towards Om Parvat, waiting for the clouds to scatter. Along the path we have seen nature in her elemental beauty and primal fury. Now we do not wish to miss her miraculous aspect. The rarified surroundings and the accompanying excitement make us forget the trivial facets of the journey. But Kiran comes up looking quite angry: 'My ponywallah left me and went somewhere. I came alone all the way. He should be scolded.' The others try to lighten her mood by diverting her attention to the scenic view around, to no avail. She comes back to the subject repeatedly, the pitch of her voice gets higher as the discussion continues.

Lunch comes as a welcome break in this cold camp. Gloves and heavier coats are out. Our armed companions have brought letters for their colleagues posted here. One jawan receives a *rakhi*, a sister's symbolic gift to her brother, sent a month ago. Naina, the woman of the noisy and jolly couple, plays the role of the sister and ties it on his wrist. He is touched and insists on giving her the sister's due.

The sky has been cloudy all day and by 5 p.m. it begins to rain heavily. Earlier we have had heavy rains only during the nights. The days have generally passed well, but today when we need a clear sky for a vision of the mountain, we are poured over. We wade through ankle-deep water to the doctor's tent for our routine inspection. Dinner is served in the tents, and the boys run back and forth with steel *thalis* and bowls of food.

They smile through the drenching waters. It is pitch dark by 6 p.m. An hour later, we are called out to see the Om Parvat. As I rush out my foot goes into a large puddle of water; the shoes which I have diligently kept dry are soaked through. A kitchen hand takes them away and dries them in front of the fire.

The sight of a luminous Om clearly inscribed in the mountain is amazing. The clouds still envelop much of the mountain and hide the tail of the symbolic letter, yet the Om stands out. Had I been told by someone about a perfect Om etched out in snow on the flank of a whole mountain, I would have found it hard to believe. But here it is, clear as crystal even in the dim light of a cloudy night. The contours of the mountain are such, that even when it snows heavily the area around the symbol remains uncovered. It is as though most of our sacred signs have been taken by sages from nature herself. The visible as well as the audible ones are all there to be experienced directly in these mountains.

Soon, our tent for seven women yatris is flooded with water. As the flaps have not been stretched taut, they collect water and sag in. There is a risk of the sleeping bags getting soaked. We try to find dry spaces in other tents, but these too are wet and the occupants are huddled in the small dry sections. Lalit Mohan and an ITBP jawan come and erect a small barrier of mud to save the small dry patch which can take two sleeping bags. It feels like sleeping in some ancient ruins on a thunderous night.

We should start at 3.30 a.m. to make it to Lipu by 7.30. After eight o'clock in the morning, Lipu is said to be covered in mist. Also, if we are not at the top of the pass when the returning group arrives, the Chinese guides are capable of leaving us and going away. And sometimes when it has snowed, pieces of baggage have been lost forever. I suggest that the yatris who have decided to walk should start early, while those on animal back may follow a little later. But the commander insists we start out together. I decide not to argue with our guides and planners. We can neither afford to lose precious equipment, nor can we allow ourselves to be left high and dry on the pass.

Over the Pass

> Imagine him [the pilgrim] travelling through gorges, where stones are falling from invisible heights and where waterfalls seem to rush down straight from the clouds. Imagine him negotiating overhanging cliffs on narrow mountain paths and sharp-edged rock-ledges which cut into sore and tired feet. Imagine all this, and see him finally on the top of the Lipu Lekh Pass, wrapped in the icy mists of its perpetual summer cloud-cap.
>
> Lama Anagarika Govinda
> *The Way of the White Cloud*

We are served hot tea in the wet dark of the night at 3 a.m. Most of us have slept little. Sandeep and Satyam have been more soaked than others. The air is damp and it is freezing cold. The ponywallahs seem to be scattered about, the guides are asleep in their tents and the jawans are nowhere to be seen. I wake Lalit Mohan who has decided to follow us later.

Many of the mules, probably left untethered, are lost as they strayed on the path leading back to Kalapani in the middle of the night. The porters and mulewallahs have spent the night out in the open due to inadequate accommodation. However, by 4 a.m. most animals are rounded up and the yatris begin to move. My mulewallah is nowhere to be seen. I stand alone surrounded by mountain silhouettes, waiting for Man Singh. He appears briefly, takes hold of my backpack and camera only to disappear again into the darkness. The silent outlines of the rocks and the sound of water breaking on stones create a strange sense of tranquillity. An ITBP man approaches me. He is a newcomer and has no idea of how to help me. He carries no torch either, so I lend him mine. He also disappears. The wait in the peace and the protection of the massive mountains is soothing. The other yatris, somewhat irritated and tense at being soaked and then having to start out early, have gone.

I rend the sacred silence by calling out to Man Singh, but get no answer. His fully saddled mule has wandered off into the dark. Even the ITBP man is lost. A few minutes later a torchlight flashes. A ponywallah appears, Man Singh has sent him to take me to Lipu as he himself has gone in search of Samli. My camera and the backpack containing the group's identification papers and vivifying remedies are all with him. 'He will catch up with you at Lipu,' says the man. With or without the goods, I must continue the journey. I get on the mount.

The steady thud of the horse's hoofs is amplified in the silence. The path is lit by the narrow beam of a torch. The stream sounds close by. Animal and man both seem to know the route instinctively. We ford waters which can only be heard. There is a vague perception of huge massifs looming in the darkness. The air is chilly, the silence penetrating. The warbling sound of water heightens the serenity. As the shadows start to lighten, a ravaged, bare landscape begins to emerge. The heavy tinkling of pony-bells is mingled with the sound of water nearby.

We move for about an hour and a half without saying a word. I do not know if I was dozing or in a reverie, but suddenly I notice snow all around. The whiteness on flat ground radiates a sense of purity. There is enchantment in the scene. As we are now at the top of the range, there are not many rocky protuberances around. On the flat, slightly undulating ground it is a wonder that our guides and companions know which way to go. We move alongside the thick communication cable laid out by the ITBP. It will be removed when we return. Without it we could easily stray off the path. Our arrival and departure from all points is telegraphed to the headquarters. Helicopters can be commissioned right up to Kalapani in case of an emergency. But the landing of a helicopter is contingent on the weather. The close mountain ranges coupled with bad visibility have led to crashes in the recent past; sometimes it is difficult to fly high enough to cross the mountain ranges.

The glow of the morning sun brings out the gleam in the snow. The journey has been faster than expected. It is a little after six when I reach the top. Despite three pairs of socks and a pair of thick gloves my hands and feet are frozen. The flaky drizzle, piercingly cold, is kept at bay by the water-resistant jacket and trousers that were thoughtfully lent by a friend.

The height makes my mind feel light and joyful. I ask the ponywallah where the medical tents are. He points, but there is nothing to be seen. It takes a while before I make out white tarpaulins stretched flat on the ground. They merge with the snow. I did not realize that we would actually have to erect the tents for our use. Three or four persons who had decided to ride have also arrived. They look blue from the cold. Soon big-built Sandeep, comes up shivering uncontrollably atop his pony. His morale seems low and fear is written across his face. He was drenched during the night and now the heightened altitude makes him colder still. The lack of oxygen makes bodily responses much slower. One of the porters informs us that the walkers are far behind, not halfway up yet. I catch sight of a frozen Rudra drenched to the skin despite adequate gear, bones rattling as audibly as human bones possibly can, looking faint. Narendra and the ITBP medical assistant rub him hard using alcohol, with little result. Besides the actual physical difficulty of breathing, it is the sense of panic that makes it harder. Will we make it?.

We push some of the yatris into a tent as soon as it is erected. Strange that at this point my own sagging, suffocating body has somehow recovered. I am able to move about and help in the administration of remedies to collapsing fellow-travellers. Homeopathic medicines, chocolates, electral, all come in handy. Besides physical rejuvenation it is necessary to keep up the morale. Surendra begins a chant of *Om Namah Shivaya.* Others take up the refrain while performing some on-the-spot exercises to keep warm. Narendra rubs some of the yatris with alcohol obtained from an ITBP man. The energy and presence of mind of these two goes a long way in boosting the spirits and the drooping bodies.

An ITBP man comes in to say that five of the stalwarts who had insisted on walking are totally exhausted, and unless they are fetched up on mules they will not make it. They are two kilometres behind. The distance is far longer than it would be on lower heights. It is difficult to round up ponywallahs who are willing to go and bring them. With some coaxing and the carrot of a few extra rupees, five of them agree to go. At about 7.30 the exhausted yatris are brought up. But Satyam, the trekker, is still missing. Fortunately, a quarter of an hour later, he painfully drags himself towards the tents, gasping heavily. He will not even make it to the Pass, a steep ten-minute ride ahead. After the administration of our energizing potions, he shows signs of recuperation but collapses again. He will have to be carried on horseback.

At this point it becomes clear that all preconceived notions about our personal identities are being eroded. Each of us is being stripped down to the core human level as coatings of wealth, position or muscle strength are peeled off. Trekkers have shown themselves to be less resilient than they thought, while the flabby yatris propelled by ritual belief, hold on well. Social differences governed by hierarchical ideas of money or position have no meaning here. What counts is the ability to cope with the elemental forces that are indifferent to our misery or joy, wealth or poverty. The mental and physical responses that emerge reflect our bare personalities. These will determine whether fears and anxieties will take the upper hand or courage based on faith will dominate. The latter enables connection with others and the surroundings. We are in the process of facing our second mental transformation. Possibly we can realize that it is our inner selves that finally deal with difficult situations in life.

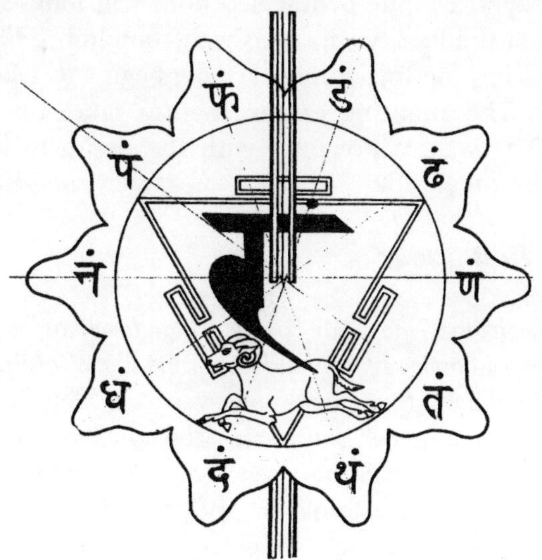

Manipura Chakra.

Devi

In the second chapter of the Devi Mahatmyam, the devatas give of their essential energies, freed of the conditionings of personality. These 'pure' energies come together to take a female form and appear as the Devi who is all-powerful. She represents the essential being-ness. Swami Venkatesananda writes in The Cosmic Dance:

. . . when the mask is lifted from the personality what you see within is Divine, the Self, which is unchanged by anything that you did or did not do. It is like space. However heavily this space is polluted, in a little while it will become completely free as it ever was, as it has always been.

Sethuram stands at the top of the Pass trying to spot the returning party. At 7.30 we get a signal indicating that the group is coming up. We start our ascent up to the Pass. The zigzag path on the white ground cover, traversed by more than 30 horses and mules carrying baggage and people is a majestic sight. Despite bedraggled bodies, it looks like a royal caravan. At the Pass, we have to wait some more till the other group reaches the top. Euphoria now begins to take the place of panic. The chanting of the mantra takes on a frenzied quality. The wait is pregnant with the desire to know what lies on the other side.

The first view

Tibet from the Lipu Lekh Pass is magnificent as, amidst all the other beauties of the landscape, the centre of the picture is occupied by four peaks, all over 22,000 ft, which are quite close together, the highest being Gurla Mandhata, 25,350 ft. This solid mass lends a grandeur to the whole which is quite awe-inspiring, and on all sides the most beautiful coloured rocks heighten the effect, so that the impression on the beholder is that the scene before him is truly one of nature's grandest handiworks. There are no trees or verdure to relieve the severity, and the almost total absence of animal life adds to the feeling of intense desolation prevailing everywhere.

C.A. Sherring

Western Tibet and the British Borderland

The Pass is about four-foot wide. It is quite easy to just walk over to the other side, no barrier prevents us from doing so. Nature has no frontiers. But we wait for the Tibetans to come and guide us into their land. Our baggage sits in untidy piles on the rocks jutting around. The cold is lessened with the increase of light on the horizon. The prospect of meeting the returning group also brings up a sense of warmth. Finally, the moment arrives. The members of the returning group are greeted as long-lost friends. How did it go with them? What are the Tibetans like? An animated barrage of questions and answers is exchanged.

We are given some tips regarding the do's and dont's on the other side. Three people in their group could not make it around Kailash and two around the Lake. We are elated at the prospect of finally going 'down' to the roof of the world. About ten steps below on the other side stands a stocky figure clad in a quilted parka with the hood pulled over. The face is almost expressionless. 'This is Garry, your guide on the other side,' says Lalit Mohan whose jurisdiction ends here, and who has met his counterpart several times at this spot. I say, 'Hello, Garry.' He returns my greeting and retreats into silence. 'What do we do now?' 'Just walk down and wait for me near the horses,' he answers. He is cryptic and the voice is toneless. For him it is just a job that he has to perform.

Where Preconceptions Grow Dim

[There] . . . the ground was covered with grass, moss and fern, flowers and shrubs; dark rocks were towering above the green valley and were lost in the heavy monsoon clouds which hid the snow-peaks; while here the vivid colours and the chiselled forms of rocks and mountains stand out in brilliant clearness, divested of any trace of vegetation, like the world on the first day of creation when only heaven and earth were facing each other in primeval purity.

Lama Anagarika Govinda
The Way of the White Cloud

The sheer drop on the other side of the pass could have been better manipulated if we had ropes to hang down from, especially since the track is covered with scree. We carry the lighter backpacks as the porters and ponywallahs are a thing of the past. Besides the recorder in my belt pouch, I have the camera and essentials. Surendra helps the old lady with her small bag. He even manages to carry one of my pieces.

About a hundred metres below us, a group of horses and horsewomen are huddled under a flank of the mountain, brewing tea and gossiping animatedly. Our arrival seems to go apparently unnoticed, but they are sizing us up through the corners of their eyes and talking to each other. Garry is nowhere in sight. We make signs to ask if they would take us down. There is no reciprocal gesture of acknowledgement. Perhaps we look like zombies from another planet. The ill-fitting gear, the balaclavas ending in a cone must make each one of us a comic sight.

The group is edgy. The larger and apparently stronger men have been complaining since morning – the tents were bad, the planning worse, the start too early, and so on. At times like this, I am isolated, but Durga continues to be supportive and cheerful. Finally, Garry comes down. 'Can we ride now?' ask the tired yatris. 'No,' Garry tells me. 'Take them down another kilometre and a half and I will join you there. It is not possible for them to ride down this slope, it is too steep and treacherous.' Not very encouraging but there is no choice. Sulky discipline and a general air of discontentment is apparent, but on the whole the group holds together.

We continue our descent onto the desert plateau. There are no cavernous gorges here. The mountains have gentle slopes even though the track we manoeuvre is very steep and slippery with loose sand and pebbles. This is the path that leads us onto the highest plateau on earth, our home for the next 12 days.

On the open meadow indicated by Garry, we wait. Satyam collapses on the ground, exhausted and lifeless. The other young men also look fazed. The women, by and large, fare better. Perhaps they have a greater capacity to cope with difficulties or they are just stronger!

We spend time munching on titbits while Durga lightens the mood by offering her share to the others and cracking jokes. Soon, Garry, or Wangchen Gelek which is his real name, comes riding down at the head of a line of horses. Some are loaded with our baggage while others are meant for the compulsory ride down the mountain onto the plateau. Suitable mounts are found for each traveller. Even Narendra who has adamantly declined to ride till now is compelled to do so. Walking down the six kilometres would delay the onward journey. So there is no choice.

We ride for about an hour and a half to reach the truck parked by a glacial stream, flowing northward down from the pass. The baggage is piled haphazardly as dazed-looking travellers dismount beside it. I almost slide under the belly of the horse in the process of dismounting. I had forgotten that Tibetans tie the saddles loose. Luckily no one notices and I straighten myself up with as much dignity as I can summon. Very soon, robust-looking Tibetans start throwing our bags into the truck. Some of the packages contain delicate articles but we try to remain calm. When the last piece of baggage is thrown in, we are asked to get on.

All 29 of us seek our foothold between the bags. Sitting on the bags we feel as if we could roll off the open, moving truck any moment. As if that were not enough, about ten Tibetan porters climb in and make place for themselves between our toes and the bags. Their heavy breathing envelops us. Some yatris feel irritated by their roguish jokes and audacious demand for cigarettes. They find it unacceptable for us to be lumped together like this. But there is no choice. Luckily the ride is not long. Now we have come to be shorn of even human adjuncts because we are treated as mere creatures, moving and breathing.

The Tibetans have devised their own methods of coping with the harsh environment – they just laugh through every situation. In the days to come we see hundreds of Tibetans using transport like ours, laughing their way over bumps and boulders. They giggle childishly at shortcomings – their own and those of others – and there is no malice in their laughter. Our mental stuff is being kneaded into a pliable dough. Those who can maintain a sense of equilibrium are the ones who will go back enriched.

Journeying in these environs, Lama Anagarika Govinda wrote:

> When every detail of our life is planned and regulated, and every fraction of time determined beforehand, then the last trace of our boundless and timeless being, in which the freedom of our soul exists, will be suffocated. This freedom does not consist in being able 'to do what we want', it is neither arbitrariness nor waywardness, nor the thirst for adventures, but the capacity to accept the unexpected, the unthought-of situations of life, good as well as bad, with an open mind; it is the capacity to adapt oneself to the infinite variety of conditions without losing confidence in the deeper connections between the inner and the outer world.[1]

We are off-loaded in a desolate area where the vastness of the plateau begins to open out. We see a bus parked across a stream. Weary from the day's travel, worried about the bags left behind in the truck, we pack ourselves into the Toyota bus after wading through the icy stream coming down from Lipu. The bus is comfortable, and the Chinese driver deft at steering it. Our vehicle heaves over sand dunes and whirrs through rushing waters; the surroundings are stark. Generally, the rain-bearing clouds discharge their water on the Indian side of the Himalayas; there is very little green cover on the Tibetan side. Fine dust enters all the bodily cavities.

Garry is businesslike. He has obviously guided a large number of groups such as ours. To him we are just another conglomeration of somewhat nervous people from the other side of the mountain, with the idea of carrying out the most blessed of yatras. But crossing over the Lipu into this territory, our faith gets a little shaken as all the conveniences and familiar signs are taken away one by one. A peculiar mixture of apprehension, excitement and exhaustion is combined with a sense of having to bear up with the different treatment meted out at this end. All this as we apparently ply through nowhere.

Taklakot

The essential continues to attract despite the ravages inflicted on external, cultural symbols.

After about three and a half hours of leaving Lipu, we arrive at Taklakot. The bus drives in through the massive gates of a recently constructed building; within it are rows of rooms on either side. The truck follows us and off-loads the bags as well as several Tibetans. We enter a large room with chairs arranged against the walls. On the lintel of the doorway is an inscription in Tibetan – a quotation from the Panchen Lama appreciating of the scenic beauty of the Ngari region of western Tibet in which Kailash and Manasarovar are located. In India, this region has been known by names such as *Kailash Khanda* and *Manas Khanda,* indicating its sanctity and importance. The major mountain ranges of the Kailash-Manas region are Kailash, Gurla Mandhata which at 25,355 feet is taller than Kailash (22,028 feet), and Kanglung. The southern boundary of Ngari is bounded by the Zanskar range.

Garry disappears after telling us to sit here. Chinese tea modified with milk and sugar to suit the Indian palate is available in generous quantities. The girl who serves it says the customs and immigration officials will come at 4 p.m. It is only twelve noon by my watch. It takes me a while to realize that though we have travelled almost directly north from Delhi, the time differs by three and a half hours the moment we cross Lipu. In Taklakot it is almost 3.30 p.m. Outside, the sun is approaching its zenith as it would at noon. But time here is the same as in Beijing, which is located about 3,000 kilometres to the east.

Electricity comes on at 10 p.m. for three hours; the television set also comes alive to connect this far-flung area with the rest of China. At other times, this region carries on in its own somnolent way unconcerned with far away cities. Soon the officials arrive and I am called up to present the group visa. The travellers are asked to 'check-in', one by one, with their passports and baggage. The process is simple, the officials friendly. They do not worry about examining the bags. There is an air of formal politeness.

Garry shows us the rooms – blocks of ten beds each, divided into two sets with one room having three, and another, two beds. Toilets, pits dug in the ground, are located more than 200 yards away. Water is available only at restricted times, and all of us must finish bathing within two hours because electricity is scarce. Other facilities provided for daily chores are peculiar at first sight. Rows of beer bottles filled with water are placed in front of the rooms, the Chinese way of recognizing the Indian propensity for ablutions.

At 4,300 metres above sea level, Taklakot is the first township across the Indian border. It is the headquarters of the dZong, the district official of Purang, and is located at a distance of 18 kilometres from Lipu Lekh Pass. It is supposed to be a military township. The word *kot* means a fort. But very little construction is visible above the ground as most structures are built either underground or in mountain cavities. The Purang (pronounced Burang, Bulang or Phulan according to speaker's linguistic background) guesthouse where we are housed is at the foot of a mountain. On its summit is visible a vast ruin. The broken-down walls do not seem to be the result of ravages wrought by time or the elements. What was this structure? Who lived in it? What was it used for? The picturesque and strategic location of the structure arouses my curiosity. We soon learn that this is the famous Simbling Gompa (Indians often call it Shivling gompa) about which much has been written by travellers. Swami Pranavananda describes it as 'the most famous lamasery . . . the biggest monastery of this region.'[1] It housed 170 monks when he saw it. Of those, six were lamas and the rest *dabas*, or trainee monks. A regular school was held here for the junior monks of the monastery, which overlooks the river Karnali and the village of Taklakot. The wandering Swami who spent several years in this region further writes:

> In the main image-hall of the monastery there is a big gilded image of the Buddha about six feet high, seated on a high pedestal, with butter-lamps burning in the front. Just before entering the image hall is the general congregational hall, festooned with scroll paintings; and the walls are decorated with fine mural paintings. Once in a year there are general feasts, merry-making, mystic or symbolic dances by the monks, lasting for a week or two. In the symbolic dance they wear long gowns and a variety of masks of different deities and animals.[2]

Apparently, the gompa housed an enormous library of Tibetan books on various practical and esoteric subjects. The Swami's description says: 'There is a separate image-hall of the "Menlha" (god of medicine) adjacent to the library halls. There are more than 400 excellent "thankas" or banner paintings and four huge silk banners of Buddha and Maitreya each measuring 60 by 30 feet.' [3] The medical manuals were spared when all the religious texts were destroyed during the cultural revolution.

The Swami goes on to explain that the monastry was affiliated to the Drepung monastery near Lhasa, which was founded in A.D. 1416. It was modelled after the Shree Dhanyakataka University situated near the Amaravati Stupa in India. All gompas were affiliated to one of the larger monasteries. The mind boggles to think of the magnitude, and the power these monasteries would have had. It is like seeing the ravages of a massive citadel.

In 1959, there were three major monasteries in Lhasa which, according to A. Tom Grunfeld:

> . . . held 16,500 monks (Drepung 7,700; Sera 5,500 and Ganden 3,300). Their power lay not only in their size but in their influence. Each 'parent' monastery was in charge of dozens, if not hundreds of 'children' monasteries. The 'parent' provided operating funds, trained elites to govern, and the 'children' membership in a powerful institution. In return the smaller monasteries extended the power and trade capabilities of the 'parent' into remote areas, while supplying shelter and guards for the carrying out of that trade.[4]

Today, all that remains of Simbling Gompa are ruined, jagged walls standing pathetically on top of a mountain. The visual of the massive and grand structure in Swami Pranavananda's book make the remaining walls a more poignant reminder of its bygone glory.

Taklakot, together with the Kailash-Manasarovar region, comes under the jurisdiction of the Ngari province of western Tibet. The administrative system of the Dalai Lama was severe, it has been stated. Viceroys or Garpons were appointed directly from Lhasa for a term of three years. A special officer called Kashyap visited western Tibet every 30 to 35 years to look into and settle disputes. The Governor's headquarters were on top of the hill together with the monastery. Simple offences were meted out with heavy torture and punishment, some leading to death. Instruments of torture were kept hanging outside the gates of the governing official's house. One monk, named Serka-Mutup, who organized an agitation to stop *begari,* or free labour, to the monastery, was whipped to death by the *Labrang* (the general managing body) of the Simbling Gompa in 1943, writes Swami Pranavananda. Other offenders were often hurled down the steep hill.[5]

High up on the sheer mountain face we can see numerous cave-like openings. They do not appear to be natural hollows or the outcome of erosions; nor could there have been so many sages inhabiting them in times gone by. But they do raise a question to which there is no answer yet.

The guesthouse, like the surroundings, is desert-like. But a variety of flowers have been cultivated in a part of the courtyard to provide a semblance of greenery. There is also a small green house in which vegetables and herbs are grown.

Dinner will be served at 8 p.m. we are told. The lightness in the head, seemingly caused by the altitude and the excitement of being here, prevents us from resting. Besides, the feeling of being constantly watched by the ruins above is oddly disconcerting. At 8 p.m. Chinese time, there is no call for dinner. Having had no meal since 3 a.m. we are now tired and hungry. The bell for dinner finally goes off an hour later – apparently the Tibetans follow time an hour earlier than the Chinese. The instructions were given according to Tibetan time, and we discover that Tibetan and Beijing time are used interchangeably here.

Dinner consists of delicately cooked Chinese food. In this remote part of the country where nothing is available, all requirements are transported from faraway markets. Yet, the Chinese cook serves up different delicacies at every meal – button or Chinese mushrooms, bamboo shoots, litchis, small peeled mandarins in syrup, various types of noodles, fried potatoes that are sweetened, and steamed Tibetan dumplings called momos. At times, the cook makes dry spiced potatoes to titillate the stronger Indian taste. Soup is generally spicy. Sweet and salty dishes are served together. There is one serving per person of all the items at each table. If someone comes late or those who share the same table have not been thoughtful, the person will be left with nothing. The quantities cooked are exact and laid out all at once. It appears that the

Tibetan and Chinese officials who look after us eat a relatively frugal meal.

We meet Garry at 10 p.m. to work out the division of the yatris into two groups for the *parikramas.* Garry has a readymade programme which he hands out to each member. Apart from the dates and time, he has drawn a map to make the locations clear. We calculate the expenses based on the number of horses, yaks and guides required for each group.

The money for the circumambulations and our board and lodging is to be paid in the morning. After the transaction, we go into the town. Garry takes us first to the Quogom gompa on the other side of the river. The entrance resembles the mouth of a cave hollowed out in the sheer rock face, and it is approached by steep zigzag steps. Before entering the monastery we step into a little room on the left. A brass prayer wheel about eight feet high and three feet in diameter fills the room. The rotation of prayer wheels is considered auspicious by the Tibetans; this is believed to spread good vibrations for the benefit of all. Garry thinks the inscription on this wheel is in Sanskrit, he knows it is not Tibetan. But it is not Sanskrit either; it looks like a script in between the two. Tibetan language is related to the Burmese and Thai languages. During the reign of King Songtsen Gampo, a script for the language was devised in A.D. 649. The king had sent his minister, Thonmi Sambhota, to study in India. On his return Sambhota formulated a script for the Tibetan language based on Devanagari characters and their arrangement.[6]

On the walls are paintings of the Buddha, and photographs of the young Dalai Lama (together with the Panchen Lama, Mao Tse Dong and Chou En Lai), before he had to flee the land. I wonder if it is considered undesirable to hang photographs of the Dalai Lama. 'Of course not': Garry gives a surprised look. We are aware that some gompas are now being refurnished after the Cultural Revolution.

A few more steps and we enter the monastery. There are big rooms inside with a look of faded grandeur about them; they must have been richly decorated earlier. All that remains now are some utensils for ritual purposes and daily use. We see a couple of lamas and one or two child-monks. A vertical tunnel in the rock leads to a small hatch in the roof accessible by a ladder. In the upper section is a narrow balcony which opens on to a rock promontory and commands a clear view of the mountains around and the valley below. Through a small door we enter a hall bedecked with massive thangkas and a large statue in bright red and black, a representation of the protecting deity.

Tibetan Buddhism abounds with gods, goddesses and spirits that ward off evil. Animism and Shamanism find a place alongside the Buddhist doctrine in Tibet. To an outsider, says Giuseppe Tucci, it could appear that 'the entire spiritual life of a Tibetan is defined by a permanent attitude of defence, by a constant effort to appease and propitiate the powers he fears.'[7] According to Tom Grunfeld, the Tibetan's strong belief in the supernatural was a result of the land's harsh climate, its almost complete isolation from the rest of the world and the consequent lack of scientific knowledge combined with the high incidence of early mortality.[8] He attributes the low doorways and high stairs in Tibetan homes to the belief in spirits. It was believed that if a dead body was not provided with proper rituals the 'soul may re-enter the body and run wild.' It was to prevent these 'reactivated corpses from chasing a living being'[9] that these measures were taken.

The altar in the shrine is lit with hundreds of butter-lamps. On the shelves built into the walls are manuscripts of sacred books wrapped in coloured silk. There are innumerable caves adjacent to the monastery; their charred walls and roofs indicate habitation in the recent past. One of the caves is supposed to have been the palace of a tribal king who fled with his people during the Cultural Revolution.

Next we walk down past a bridge over the Karnali, through the Nepali *mandi,* which was once an active trade centre. Swami Pranavananda mentions the *mandi,* busy between June and October every year, on the narrow plateau called Pilithanka situated at the foot of a hillock. Indian 'Bhotia merchants of Dharma Pargana sold their goods or exchanged them directly for enormous quantities of Tibetan wool, salt, and borax.' He writes of walled enclosures made of stones or sun-dried bricks with gates, and tents set up temporarily within them. According to the treaty of 1904 between the British and the Tibetan Government, Indians were not allowed to construct roofed houses in Tibet.[10] So, when they wound up, they left their dismantled gates and unsold commodities in one of the cave dwellings.

There are mud houses on the lower side of the river and a small hospital. Across the river is a row of stalls with goods spread out on the roadside, selling oddments from neighbouring countries – cloth from India, woollens from Nepal, readymade clothes from China, caps and shoes, torches and batteries. A number of Nepalis come here on business, and they speak Hindi. Some Tibetans also speak Nepali and a little Hindi. Bargaining plays an important role in the transaction of merchandise.

Set back from the road is a community hall, and on its verandah people are playing pool, a popular Chinese pastime here. A little beyond the Nepali *mandi* is the government canteen; prices are low but there is very little that can be bought. Heavy woollen coats for about 70 yuans, wide-brimmed Tibetan hats for eight yuans. There is Coca-Cola and grape juice, large bottles of orange and lemon drinks, all from the West. We buy jerry cans for collecting Manas water, batteries and cold drinks. The men behind the counters are not very keen to sell to Indians, perhaps because they inquire too much and buy too little. Tibetans come in, buy and move off. There is not much they buy anyway. There are inscriptions in Chinese and red flags everywhere in the compound of the canteen.

Back at the guesthouse music blares constantly from a loudspeaker. Most of the songs are in Chinese, some are Tibetan songs translated into Chinese. Once in a while the music is interrupted for what sounds like a harangue in Chinese, probably information about developments in the area. The

Chinese girls at the Purang guesthouse do not respond to our questions; they just turn away with a blank look.

When we entered Tibet from Lipu we had noticed a number of traditionally clad men, mostly in rags, carrying a small bag hung on a bamboo pole. We learn that they are proceeding towards Kailash, and that this is a special year according to the Tibetan calendar. In 1027, Pandit Somnath of Kashmir translated the *Kala Chakra Jyotisha* into Tibetan and introduced the *Brihaspati* cycle of 60 years to the land. This cycle of 60 years is divided into five sub-cycles of 12 years each. Each of the years in this calendar is given a particular name drawn from a combination of the five elements: fire, earth, iron, water, and wood; and 12 animals: hare, dragon, serpent, horse, sheep, monkey, hen, dog, pig, mouse, ox and tiger.[11] The name of each year is associated with one element and one animal. Once every 12 years, the horse comes together with one of the elements. The year of the horse is looked upon with great reverence and is considered auspicious. This year, the horse has come together with iron. This combination which occurs once in 60 years is especially auspicious. Kailash *parikramas* performed in such a year have greater significance: each *parikrama* is considered to be as effective as 13 of those performed ordinarily. Therefore, vast numbers of people from different areas have converged onto Taklakot on their way to the north.

The Twin Lakes

The lower urges and higher aspirations are both manifestations in the One that underlies everything.

We are ready at 7 a.m. Chinese time, to start for Dharchen and Houre, one located at the base of Kailash and the other on the northeastern side of Manasarovar. Two groups of yatris have been formed, and baggage divided into four sections, two for each group. One set of bags will be carried by each group during the circumambulations of Kailash and Manasarovar. The rest will remain at the base camp in Dharchen for the second *parikrama*. The bags are systematically loaded into a truck, while we get into the bus for the final leg of our onward journey.

Stars shine brilliantly against a clear sky; the actual time according to us is 3.30 a.m. It will take a while before we get used to the unpolluted environment, in which starlight filters through with clarity. The bus heaves and rolls like a ship on rough seas. We are back on the pathless path; only the driver knows the route. The wind becomes chillier as we roll and bump along. From the dimly-lit interior of the bus, the outside appears pitch dark but once in a while, silhouettes of dark massifs are visible. We go past the Gurla Mandhata Range. Two and a half hours later the sky begins to lighten. We are able to discern the contours of Gurla Mandhata, the highest mountain in the region. Every now and then, we spot some Tibetans returning from their pilgrimage. A dull stupor overtakes us because none of us knows how long the 104-kilometre journey will take. Suddenly we hear a high-pitched call from Surendra – 'Kailash!' We come awake with alacrity to watch the snow-white mountain reveal itself in absolute fullness. The purity of the cloudless vision is overwhelming, as though our *tapas* has been rewarded with the *darshan* of a living deity. A spontaneous chorus *Kailashpati Mahadev Ki Jaya* reverbrates through the interior of the bus.

Something wells up within me. My heart performs an involuntary *abhishekam.* Barriers melt, it is difficult to maintain a social composure. A few minutes later, the bus comes to a halt. We disembark by the side of a clear, ripple-free lake. Kailash gleams from across its large expanse. The lake is serene, silently filling herself with a morning vision of the sacred form. The atmosphere is calm and harmonious, as if the elements have stretched themselves out to their barest, almost translucent form. The complexities of vegetation are absent here. With our psychological conditioning put into question, we too, are in a more fitting state of mind to face the unadorned and the natural.

The mountain stands in pristine clarity, its luminosity making the hardness of the rock appear ethereal. We soak in the vision through brimming eyes. Some walk up closer to the lake, others kneel down and prostrate themselves on the earth. It feels like sacrilege to lift a camera and point it at this magnificent and sacrosanct entity.

The expanse of water that separates us from the mountain is Rakshasa Tala, or Ravana Hrida, so named because Ravana, the ten-headed demon king of Lanka in the *Ramayana,* is said to have performed *tapas* here for a thousand years. In his youth, Ravana had pleased Brahma by severe austerities in which he offered one head after another. When he was about to cut off his tenth and last head, Brahma appeared and reinstated all his heads, giving him the boon of a long and mighty life. Ravana then challenged his half brother, the gentle Kubera who ruled over Lanka. Kubera left the kingdom to Ravana and set up a city equalling that of Indra in beauty and grandeur at Alkapuri near Kailash. This city glittered with gems and gold and valuable herbs.[1] Ravana followed his brother here too, and appropriated Kubera's aerial vehicle, the *Pushpak Vimana* which had amazing capabilities and was bedecked with the rarest of gems and jewels. As Ravana flew in the *Pushpak Vimana*, he found his way blocked by a high mountain – the Kailash. Annoyed at this obstruction, Ravana decided to lift the mountain and carry it with him. As he slipped his arm under the mountain, its movement made Parvati fearful. So, Shiva playfully pressed the mountain with the toe of one foot to hold it there. An agonized Ravana prayed to Shiva, singing and chanting the most beautiful *shlokas* in his praise, asking for release. After a thousand years, a pleased Shiva released and rewarded him with a specially crafted sword, the Chandrahasa.[2]

Hindus consider the water of this lake inauspicious due to its association with Ravana. In Tibetan the lake is called *Langak Tso*, the lake in which there are five mountains, or a lake which has five mountains drowned in it (*La*: mountain; *nga*: five; *tso*: lake). The topography of the area is such that the mountains around are reflected perfectly in it. Located about seven kilometres west of Manasarovar, this lake is larger with a circumference of about 115 kilometres as against 86 kilometres of the sacred lake.[3] The morning sun gleams on the waters even as it etches out the luminous contours of Kailash against the cloudless sky.

A little further north, Rakshasa Tala is connected to Manasarovar by a stream known as Ganga Chhu through which waters from the sacred lake flow into this one. The shallow stream has a span of 40 to 60 feet and a length of about 10 kilometres. A Tibetan legend has it that Rakshasa Tala was originally the abode of demons, so nobody drank its water. But it so happened that two golden fish that lived in Manasarovar had a quarrel and one pursued the other into this lake. The course taken by the fish became the Ganga Chhu and the waters of this Tala became sanctified by an inflow of water from the Manasarovar. Since then the water of this lake is not taboo for the Tibetans. However, the water is still considered inauspicious by Hindus. The Tibetans do not have any monasteries around this lake, though Swami Pranavananda mentions the existence of one on its north-western corner.

There was no water in the Ganga Chhu for several years, which according to Tibetans is an ill omen. But since one year, a trickle running through it portends better times as 'mother and father' are supposed to be in harmony. The river Sutlej begins from the west of this lake and takes a south-westerly route to enter the Indian subcontinent. No river flows out of Lake Manasarovar today, but the facts may have been otherwise in the past. At one time, the two lakes were one with an island in the centre.[4] The *Skanda Purana* predicts that in Kaliyuga the spread of Manasarovar will decrease as mountains take the place of the waters.[5] The waters are a remnant of the great ice sheet which covered all of Tibet and the land up to Siberia during the ice age. Geologically speaking, the sand around them is very new; it consists of the debris from the upper crust of the earth's surface when it crunched due to the collision of the two plates. The ancient and the newborn exist side by side in this land of Shiva even as they become symbols for reflecting the change that unfolds ceaselessly.

Unwillingly, we scramble back into the bus after this short break. A quiet descends in the bus as though any sound from us would taint the sanctified surroundings. We gaze unblinkingly at the white dome. The heart irresistibly flows out in obeisance. From behind, someone moves forward to where I am seated. It is Mankad. 'Oh, I am so grateful for having been brought here,' he murmurs as though an agency other than himself were responsible for that. All I can do is to let my own feeling melt into the warmth of his. We are bound in a common act of involuntary oblation. Gratitude forms part of the inner offering.

Rudra compulsively begins to chant the names of Shiva. Joyfully, we start thinking of the numerous synonyms for the god: *Ghana*, *Kutastha*, *Tapasvi*, *Ghora*, *Rudra*, *Maheshwara*, *Sthanu*, and so on. He recites the *Shiva Manas stotram.* His melodious voice soon turns liquid with emotion.

Just a few minutes later we are on the sacred shores of the Manasarovar. This is our first close view of the lake; we had only had a glimpse of it as we drove here. Surrounded by a vast desert and bare mountains it does look like an 'emerald set in platinum'. The shape is somewhat oval, almost round, with smooth edges unlike the jagged and dramatic Rakshasa Tala. It is considered by some Hindus to be one of the *Shakti Peethas*, a place where the Devi herself resides in her physical aspect. We view it from Tseti. We are told that some of the ashes of Mahatama Gandhi's body were immersed here. We notice a pole with flags strung diagonally on all sides. One flag holds an inscription made by the group that preceded us. Tripathiji wants a ritual bath in the holy water. It is early and a bit cold. Besides, we must go on to Dharchen, the base of the beckoning mountain where half the group will be off-loaded; the other half goes to the other side of Manas, from where our *parikrama* around the lake will begin. Oblations to the rising sun are made with the sacred water. Naina relates how Shiva and Parvati just came to her in the form of two Tibetan pilgrims, only to disappear, leaving behind a jerry can full of water. For some reason she did not pick up the can to preserve it as a memento.

The twin lakes seen as the two eyes of a living being, are like a miracle in this desert land. There is no indication to suggest the sudden appearance of two such large bodies of water. The symbiotic existence of contrasting natural phenomena seems to play a role in making this region sacred and sometimes magical. The lakes also represent the two opposing forces that govern existence, light and darkness. Drawn from the word *manas*, the name Manasarovar stands for the mind or consciousness, the innate capacity and aspiration of human beings to reach out to a higher goal. Rakshasa Tala represents the basal force, the substratum from which the higher psychic forces arise. The two are symbols of the chakras in the human body, the lower forces at the bottom of the spinal column and those associated with consciousness at the crown of the head. However, the two remain connected to form the whole.

The Rakshasa Tala is set in a landscape of startling beauty at the base of Kailash, receiving its waters directly from the Mountain. It is connected to the holy Lake through the thin column of Ganga Chu. Though isolated and uninhabited as no one built monasteries around it, it represents a fundamental fact of existence. It proclaims that those which are seen to be the lower forces are as much a manifestation of the Divine as those we reckon to be the higher urges. It is, thus, not out of keeping that Rakshasa Tala receives a continuous benediction from both the mountain and the Lake. It is from the existential darkness of non-knowing that the knowledge of the Supreme arises. As Lama Anagarika writes, 'The one is the root and foundation of all our inner forces, the other the blossom and fruit of realization. The one stands at the beginning, the other at the end of spiritual evolution.'[6] While the jagged contours of the Rakshasa Tala do not allow a *parikarma* to be performed around it, the Manasarovar standing alone and open in the midst of unreachable mountain ranges envelopes the yatri in its tranquil environment as one circumambulates its waters and savours its beauty from all sides.

Golden Sands

All the mountains imagined Himalaya to be the calf
And Sumeru mountain to be the milkman
Thus they milked the earth of precious and luminous gems and medicinal herbs.

Kalidasa
Kumarasambhavam

The sand here is of an orange-yellow colour, especially so on the isthmus between Rakshasa Tala and Manasarovar. The area is known as Golden Sands. Gold has actually been found here – the Tibetans say the biggest lump was the size of a dog. Of course it is left to us to imagine the actual mass of the animal's body. As nobody dared to keep that massive lump of gold, it was taken to the Dalai Lama at Lhasa. When the Dalai Lama learned where it came from, he sent it back to be buried in the same place. Tibetans believed that anything found in this sacred soil belonged to the gods. It is said that a small stupa was built where the huge piece of gold was buried. We do not see any sign of it along the route we take.

According to another Tibetan myth, the fourth Panchen Lama deputed a man to bring two sacks of sand from the Lake all the way to Tashi Lumpo, the seat of the Panchen Lama. The distance to be covered was about 1500 kilometres. The man perceived the order as a whimsical, crazy idea of a senile old man. So he carried back only one sack. Back in Tashi Lumpo pure gold poured out of the sack. After his death, the statue of the Panchen Lama was carved out of that gold.[1] The gold was said to be purer than any found elsewhere.* A number of travellers and pilgrims have written of their encounters with dacoits and bandits in the region.

Even the *Mahabharata* records the valuable gifts brought by the kings of the region that lay between the Meru and Mandarachal mountains, when they went to attend the Rajasuya Yagya performed by Yudhishthira at Indraprastha. Among the articles they brought were *chanwars* (black and white whisks made from yak's tails) and special *madhu*, honey drawn from the rare flowers and herbs of the area. They also brought mounds of gold that had been drawn out by ants![2] A similar description was apparently given by Herodotus as well when he said that in a great desert north of India, nuggets of gold were thrown up by large ants as they burrowed into the ground.

The mystery of these statements was solved by Nain Singh when, about 1864, he reached north of the Indus, surveying Tibet for the British government in India. Going past small piles of earth that looked like ant hills, on the fabled goldfield of Thok Jalung, further north and west from Manasarovar, he

---

* M.N. Deshpande, ex-Director General, Archaeological Survey of India, saw gold being collected from the sands of the Indus, in its lower reaches, when he visited Attock (October to December 1944) to see the place where Alexander the Great had crossed river Indus. He says:

There we (I and Dr. M. Dixit) saw two persons in knee-deep water doing something. We approached them and found that they were collecting particles of gold from the sands, which they were washing with water. They were picking small sparkling, very tiny atoms by means of tongs.

found a number of miners living 'more or less permanently underground.' They sometimes covered themselves with dark coloured yak skins. Nain Singh recorded it as the coldest place he had ever visited, with a chilling wind blowing ceaselessly across the 17,000-foot plateau. The goldminers stayed below the ground, pitching tents inside their digs to avoid this wind. They slept in a most extraordinary position: drawing their knees close up to their heads and resting themselves on their knees and elbows, placing every scrap of clothing available on to their backs. Even in this condition Nain Singh found them to be cheerful and 'always ready to break into a song'. Despite their crude methods, they dug up great quantities of gold for 'even as he watched Nain Singh saw unearthed a nugget weighing more than two pounds'.[3]

The region is also rich in precious stones and gems. Coral from here has been an important article of trade. Small statues of various deities, especially Ganesha, have often been carved in coral. In the third and fourth centuries B.C., coral was imported into India from the Mediterranean region. But in the medieval period when the route between India and Tibet became known, large-sized corals were brought into India from here. Kumaoni ladies were rarely without some coral jewellery. It is in recognition of this fact that the *Brahmanda Purana* describes Kailash as glittering with a variety of gems and minerals. 'It resembled the sun at midday and had the lustre of molten gold. It had stairs built of diamonds and crystals, with steps of rocky surfaces of variegated forms. It was full of gold and was divinely variegated on account of different kinds of minerals.'[4] The spiritual was not seen to be devoid of material beauty and the splendour of wealth.

Towards Kailash

From here the journey is almost directly west to Kailash, about 30 kilometres away. We witness the southern face of the mountain with its dark, horizontal striates that look like the *tripunda* – the three lines drawn across the forehead – with

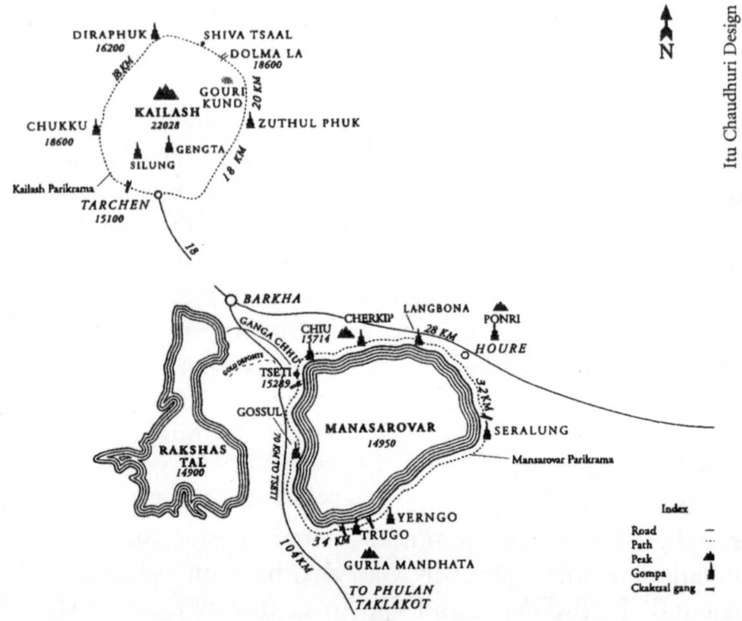

Impressionistic map of Kailash-Manasarovar.

which Shiva worshippers identify themselves. The lines are representative of the God who governs *kala,* or time, as well as manifest life. The peculiar conical shape of the snow-covered mountain, with its dark gullies that remain bereft of snow even in the deepest of winter, give it a unique character, a personality, according to Lama Anagarika. The dark notches in the rock have also been looked upon as a stairway to heaven. During the summer months when the plains around it are bare, Kailash stands like a mammoth crystal dominating the surrounding vastness.

Christian missionaries who came here with the idea of converting Tibetans faced many unexpected hardships. Ipolito Desideri, a young Jesuit from Italy, came to Tibet in 1715; he was inspired by Father Antonio de Andrade, the first missionary to visit western Tibet in 1624. Reaching the Barkha plain from the western side Desideri wrote: 'Away from the road there stands an enormously high mountain, very wide in circumference, its summit hidden among the clouds, covered with perpetual snow and ice, and most terrible on account of the icy cold.' He had heard of Padmasambhava who had lived in a cave in the mountain and played an important role in the establishment of Tibetan Buddhism. He wrote, 'Not only do the Tibetans visit the cave, where they invariably leave some presents, but with very great inconvenience to themselves they make a round of the whole mountain, an occupation of some days, by which they gain what I might call great indulgences.'[5]

We spot gazelles now and again. Kayangs and long-haired goats with large horns also belong here. They are the source of the merino wool valued for its warmth and softness. The sacred *chanwar gai* is none other than the yak. The long bushy tail is used to make the *chanwars* for fanning sacred shrines. We notice some rabbits and wild asses and wonder where they hide themselves in the cold, and what they live on. The musk deer is also found here. Tibetans traded in musk and rock fungi together with the precious stones found here. *Shilajit* is a famous natural tonic found in the region.

The all-pervading clear light makes even the atmosphere appear luminous. Varying hues of purple, violet, magenta and other unidentifiable colours bathe the mountain. They diffuse its lines, blurring the boundaries between empty spaces and concrete substance. Nothing seems clearly defined as appearances change with the light. The colours, contours, and undulations all form part of a moving chiaroscuro.

The path now opens onto a vast meadow located between Rakshasa Tala and Kailash. Many caravan routes going north to south and east to west meet here. It is said to have been a favourite haunt of robbers and nomads. We see vast flocks of sheep and yaks herded by nomadic tribes known for their ferocious dogs. By the time winter sets in they would have moved to other regions. There are swift-flowing streams here and many swamps; the driver deftly avoids these. The pure white dome of Kailash keeps our minds and eyes engaged.

The path to Kailash is through hard sand. We go past trucks crowded with jolly, excited Tibetans who come from as far as 3,000 kilometres. We notice telecommunication poles which connect Taklakot and Dharchen and Shinjan in the west. This is the only line of communication with the outside world. Even this tenuous link is inaccessible to us when we perform the circumambulations of the two natural shrines.

The level ground is replete with subterranean volcanic activity which must radiate strong currents of energy as the suture from which this energy may be released is situated at the base of Kailash. The ions that charge the bloodstream with new electrons, spoken of by Swami Sivananda, may be the result of the emission of these subtle currents. These may also

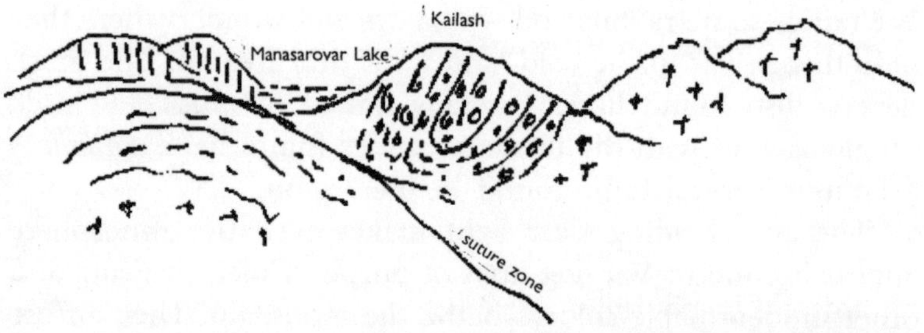

Line drawing of the suture on which the Kailash stands, by A.P. Tiwari.

be the reason for the magnetic attraction that the place has for those who reach here. The icy dome stands atop deep subterranean wells of boiling water. A little drilling could result in the gushing forth of great geysers by the immense pressure within.[6] It seems as if the serene mountain holds and restrains this cataclysmic force.

Our bus stops at a tiny township at the base of Kailash from where the *parikrama* is usually begun. A startling view of the south face of Kailash can be had from here on a clear days. Tarchen, or Dharchen, is a symbolic name, *dhar* meaning *dhvaja,* or flag, and *chhen* meaning big. The big flagstaff on the western side of Kailash, considered the gateway to the *parikrama*, is located in an open meadow about six kilometres away. This year being especially auspicious, there was a big festival here. Buddhists from various parts of the world congregated and performed a ritual to venerate the mountain.

Traditionally, Dharchen has been a wool shearing centre. Traders from the surrounding regions and countries sold their wares here. Even now a number of Tibetans, especially Khampas, come to set up shop during the yatra season.

A dusty truck is parked outside the guesthouse, a straight row of rooms, our halt before we embark on the Kailash *parikrama*. More construction is underway. A veritable village of tents has emerged in front of the guesthouse. Tibetans who have already performed the *parikrama* wait for a truck ride back to their homes.

Our baggage truck arrives with billows of dust. The systematically loaded bags in the truck are now a haphazard pile; many Tibetans along the way had taken a ride in it. We spend an hour sorting them out again, and finally the bags we are taking to Manasarovar are loaded into the bus. A number of Nepalis are keen to speak to us in Hindi; old and young, men, women and children crowd around making our arrival chaotic.

Fifteen yatris or one half of the group begins the Kailash *parikrama* from here. One room is allotted to the three women and two rooms to the 12 men. A small shop sells souvenirs, hand-woven pictures of Kailash and Manasarovar made in China with inscriptions in English, Chinese and Tibetan.

Fourteen yatris, of which I am one, form the other half of the group. We board the bus, heading eastwards to Houre on the north-east corner of Manas, from where we begin our *parikrama* of the sacred lake tomorrow. The 45-kilometre drive is part of the main route connecting this desolate western region to Lhasa. It is said that the track has been made from the material obtained by breaking down stupas. We travel for more than four hours. For a while Garry takes over the driving; having manoeuvred the vehicle across innumerable water courses, around rock boulders, sand pits and swamps, the driver gets a much-needed rest.

At Houre, we stop at a house owned by a Tibetan family; they regularly let out rooms to the yatris. The mud-walled, low-roofed rooms crowded with folding steel cots seem suffocating, but we get used to them soon. The rectangular courtyard outside has a shallow well – the only water source for our needs. In the family kitchen, two olive-skinned Tibetan women look elegantly modern in their outfit of jeans and colourfully embroidered Tibetans jackets.

Garry introduces us to Gele who will bring the horses tomorrow at 6.30 a.m; then he is off with the bus, telling us to contact him if something goes amiss. I wonder how we can possibly reach him at Taklakot, a hundred kilometres away with no means of communication. The local time at Houre is 5.30 p.m; we have to settle down and cook for ourselves before dark. The stove is strange and unfamiliar, a little carelessness can shoot a withering flame at the cook. Gele helps us with it when we make tea. Durga and Kiran, our cooks for this period, serve us a sumptuous meal of tomato rice in candlelight.

Tomorrow, a 35-kilometre walk will take us to the monastry of Quglho (also written Trugo and Qugu) located directly to the south of the lake. In two days, we walk 65 of the 86 kilometres around the lake; the rest has been covered by bus because the land is marshy and mountainous.

I take a walk outside the compound, hoping to touch the water of the Lake which is visible and doesn't seem far. But all I manage is to see the village consisting of a few mud houses, their back doors opening out to the Lake, horse dung and other rubbish littered indiscriminately all over the place. It is not possible to get near the water as the area is marshy and covered with prickly shrubs. I spot three men from our group who have also walked the same way, hoping for a bath but back without success. We will have to wait till we reach a hospitable part of the shore.

At night we tuck ourselves into warm quilts with clean covers; the low roof and thick mud walls keep out the sub-zero temperature. Once in bed, most of us are lost to the world.

Around the Lake

> Wonderful, attractive, enchanting lake ! Theme of story and legend, playground of storms and changes of colour, apple of the eye of gods and men, goal of weary yearning pilgrims, holiest of the holiest of lakes, are thou, Tso-Mavang, lake of all lakes. Navel of Old Asia . . . the pearl of all the lakes of the world.
>
> Sven Hedin
> *Transhimalaya*

By 2 a.m. Indian time there is much activity – tying up of bags, drinking tea, saying prayers – as we are to leave in an hour. With the group having become smaller and like-minded people clubbed together, the yatra seems more defined and focused. We are in a meditative mood talking about the sacred journey and our experiences till now. Tripathiji plays his recorded commentary of the yatra. He has been using his dictaphone and likes to play back his emotion-choked description of it.

It is still dark, though the stars shine brightly. Bhairavi is confused, 'Is it night or day?' She realizes that the time here is different but she is unable to come to terms with it.

It is almost 7.30 local time, but there is no sign of Gele or the horsewallahs. We are all ready and packed, though we had been warned by the preceding group to be relaxed about timings. I wait in the kitchen; the fireplace is never free of large kettles of boiling water. The ubiquitous red-coloured, gigantic thermos flasks stand in a corner, as does a drum of precious diesel. The rest of the room is filled with cots along the walls. The women seem snug in the warmth they have created. They examine my small torch; had I another I would have happily parted with this one. They are friendly and offer Tibetan tea. A Tibetan description for the rich is 'those whose lips are always moistened with tea.'[1] I feel happy at the opportunity to taste the tea which is more like thick soup with a heavy smell and taste of yak butter. The salt in it surprises the taste buds, but a few sips are enough to send a warm surge through the body. Fortified by it I feel more ready to face the cold outside.

Another half-hour goes by before one horse makes an entry through the gate in the mud wall. An old man follows and several minutes later two more amble in. They will move only when the day breaks, they say. Finally, an adequate number of horses is assembled. We count them as Garry had advised; we count the men and women also, and show them our baggage. One of the men lifts each piece, judging its weight to make small piles. Given the odd mixture of pieces the piles cannot be equal in weight. So a lottery system is devised to assign the baggage to all the men and their horses. The baggage loaded, we are provided with horses to ride on. Once a horse is allocated, each of us will have to use the same one throughout the *parikrama*.

By about 9 a.m., we are on our way. The horsemen and women insist we ride the animals. Most of us with the exception of Surendra, Naresh and Satyam comply initially. The saddles are wooden; the people in charge help us mount.

Though basically well-intentioned they are business-like and do not understand why some of us are fearful or fussy. It is not long before Vinod has a fall, the walkers rush to help him. The Tibetans find it funny but for us the experience is discouraging. We want the horsewallahs to walk alongside the riders, but they are irritated by our insistence and continue to walk far ahead.

Soon we find that our presuppositions about the ratio of horsewallahs to riders has gone awry. A horse owned by one person is not so much as touched by another. One horsewallah may have four horses while another may have only one, and the latter may be used for baggage! The person who owns the baggage-horse does not take any responsibility for a horse that carries a yatri. Bhairavi grumbles constantly, 'They walk with the younger people and not with me. There is a prejudice in favour of the young, when I am the one who needs help.'

With ten words of Tibetan at my command, I try to ask our whimsical horsewallahs to walk with her. They refuse point blank. Bhairavi turns to Satyam, 'At least you should walk with me. I am older, it is your duty to help me.' An obedient Satyam tries to get the fear out of her mind and asks her to sit up straight and tight. But she is not to be placated and after a while Satyam also tires.

As we walk southward, the east bank of the lake emerges on our right. The waters which span about 26 kilometres from one shore to another, make it appear more like a sea than a lake. The barren mountains and the shingly sands heighten the sense of solitariness. Mount Kailash becomes visible as the rays of the sun pay homage and perform a luminous *abhishekam* over the deity. In front, beyond the southern shore, stands the massive Gurla Mandhata fully clad in snow. While Kailash stands behind like a sentinel watching every step, Gurla Mandhata beckons us forward.

Gurla Mandhata is known by many names in Tibet, one of them being Memo Dang Ay, translated as 'she has two facets', sometimes beautiful and peaceful, at others storm-ridden and fierce. It is said to be the abode of the goddess who governs agriculture and rain. According to a local legend, it is prophesied that a holy man will arrive to unlock the mysteries of this mountain, making it the holiest in the region, just as a Tibetan monk did for Kailash a thousand years ago.

The Lake is a serene azure in the gentle morning light. It seems to stretch itself out in total surrender only to receive Kailash in her depths. The reflection of the mountain appears an intermingled presence, inseparable from the receiving abyss even as it changes colours with the light. The mobile, receiving lake and the still, ever-present mountain form a oneness like the eternal embrace of Demchog (the deity that represents Highest Bliss) and Dorje Phangmo (the symbolic form of transcendental knowledge) in the Tibetan pantheon. Supreme Bliss and Divine Wisdom form an inseparable duo. It is like the symbolic representation of Shiva and Shakti for the Hindus.

The paint box of light is forever at work. The surrounding mountains change colour every half-hour and their contours appear in ever-new forms. One does not realize *when* this happens, there is only a sudden awareness that the grey has turned to crimson gold. The transparent atmosphere makes the 'colours reach the eye with unfiltered intensity: rich reds, browns, yellows, purples, and in fine weather both the sky and the mirroring water are a deep, noble blue.'[2] The stillness and bareness have no counterpart in things we have known and seen. The air too bears a different quality. The right side of the body remains cold with wind from the lake while the left receives warmth from the sun. Snelling writes, 'while a man's arm, exposed to the heat of the sun, may be being scorched, his feet, lying in the shadow, may at the same time be suffering the ravages of frostbite.'[3] This must be the reason why Tibetans have devised their unique manner of carrying and wearing woollen garments. They are often seen with their jackets thrown diagonally across the body – one arm slipped through the sleeve, on the colder side, while the other sleeve dangles free under the armpit.

The white dome pervades and permeates everything – its benevolent eye is never absent. Like a central spire it appears to hold everything together. The Lake, the mountains, the humans, all seem connected in its presence.

The One That Never Gets Heated or Troubled

For the Hindus, the Lake is said to have been created by Brahma at the request of 12 pre-Vedic rishis who retired here to perform intense *tapas*. They were rewarded with a *darshan* of the Divine duo, Shiva and Parvati. When the rishis realized they had no water for daily ablutions, they prayed again to Brahma, who in his bounteousness created the Lake. Devotees walk around Manasarovar in the hope of gaining rewards in the hereafter. Its water is considered more sacred than that of the Ganga.[4]

For the Buddhists, the Lake is connected to the Buddha's descent on earth. Queen Maya (Buddha's mother) dreamt that the couch on which she slept was carried by her guardian deities to the *Anotatta* (Manasarovar) Lake. After being bathed in the sacred waters all human impurities fell away and she was ready to receive the future Buddha in her womb. The Buddha descended from the direction of Kailash, appearing like a white elephant in a cloud.[5] The word, *anotatta,* means 'that which never gets heated or troubled'.

A Tibetan myth places the origin of the Lake in an act of giving, of non-possessiveness. It is connected to a Buddha-like king named Nyngbal, who was generous and enlightened. While strolling outside his palace he once encountered four sufferings – birth, old age, disease and death. Perturbed, he approached a Brahmin and asked for a solution to these phenomena. The Brahmin told him there was no solution, but he could attain peace of mind by making big donations to the people of the world. The King gave and gave to all the people for a continuous period of 12 years. Every day rice was boiled in huge cauldrons and its water thrown in a big ditch. While there is no mention as to whether suffering ended or not, it is said that the water thus discarded became the Manasarovar. Its overflowing water became the river Ganga. Another word for the Lake is *Ma Doe*, or 'that which does not become hot'.[6] At the same time it is called *Tso Mapham*, 'the invincible one', for all the qualities of goodness that reside in it.

Both Pali and Sanskrit texts describe Manasarovar as *Anotatta* or *Anavatapta*, and they speak of fantastic things in and around it. In its centre is a tree which bears fruits that can heal all human ailments, physical as well as mental. *Anavatapta* is described as the true paradise on earth with mighty lotus flowers, some of them golden, as big as the Amitabha Buddha. The Buddha and the Bodhisattvas often sit on those flowers. It is considered the home of heavenly *rajahansas*, divine swans that feed on natural pearls and sing celestial melodies as they swim. It is also believed that a number of rivers including the Ganga flow out of the Lake. The Ganga is supposed to flow underground till it appears at Gomukh as the source of the Bhagirathi. Physically, other than the Ganga Chhu, no other water stream has been seen to flow out of the Lake.

We see a number of white geese along the shores of the Lake. There is no lotus to be seen; the trees and the golden swans remain invisible to our eyes. Perhaps they are a metaphor for the creative power of the Lake – an inner experience rather than a perception through the physical senses.

As for the aquatic birds, Swami Pranavananda categorizes three kinds in his monumental work on the Kailash Manasarovar region. There are the *ngangba,* which correspond to the traditional swan, a yellow bill with a black knob on the tip and orange legs. On its head two black horizontal bars extend from eye to eye. The upper part of the body is grey or light-ash and the lower part and the face are white. The female of the species is whiter than the male. The second variety is the *ngaru–sechung*, deep or almond-brown in colour. Its head and belly are light brown and white and the lower part of the wings, tails, legs and bill are black. The third, *chakarma* is deep grey, more like a pigeon in colour.

Its head and wings are light grey, the neck and belly white, the tip of the tail and bill black, and the bill is thin like that of a pigeon.[7] We see these colourful winged creatures as we walk along, delicate white lines are carved above the Lake as they fly together.

One of the *prasadas* carried home by pilgrims consists of dead fish thrown ashore by the waters of the Lake, also pebbles and little stones. During the winter when the upper part of the Lake is frozen, great cracks appear in its surface due to the activity of the water underneath. Sometimes great waves throw up stones that have lain at the bottom for millennia. Such pebbles are said to be charged with great energy and healing properties. Tibetans grind them and use them for medicinal purposes.

It is believed that the mountains surrounding the Lake have the *shata-mulikas*, or a hundred herbs. I cannot help thinking of Hanuman's effort to rejuvenate Lakshmana. Could it have been from this region? Kubera, the lord of herbs and other medicinal treasures, resides in these environs.

The walk is through flat ground on pebbles and low grasses. The *parikrama* of the lake is a continuous reminder of the level of transparency that can be reached by the mind if the load of agitations subsides. Two hours later we come to the Seralung gompa – large but desolate – located directly to the east of the Lake.

Gompas, Chortens and Chaktsal Gangs

External symbols and rituals only heighten the sense of omnipresence of the Divine.

Gompas, solitary dwellings for worship and shelter, are man-made structures standing in the vast emptiness. They highlight the human aspiration to delve into a depth that external forms symbolize. The gompa's small cells and terraces that open out to the vastness of the lake or the sky provide a place for meditation and intense spiritual practices. While every bit of land around the lake is sacred, some parts are considered more hallowed than others. It is on these that gompas, chortens or chaktsal gangs are located.

The solid and closed-looking shrines, with small windows cut into thick walls, merge into the surroundings. Many are built into the sides of the mountains with steep zigzag steps leading up. As in Gunji, windows are planned with care. It seems that the whole structure is built with an eye on the placement of the windows; they open out to beautiful vistas that elevate the mind.

Gompas also served as shelters for pilgrims. While the main shrine, a red-coloured structure, houses the deities the guesthouses are white-plastered rooms in straight rows. All the gompas were affliated to, and supported by, one of the main monasteries in Lhasa. Of the eight gompas around Manas, three – Cherakip, Lang-pona and Ponri – are located on the northern shores of the Lake. On the eastern side is the Seralung, to the southeast the Yerngo, and directly to the south of the Lake, facing Mount Kailash is the Trugo (or Thugolho) gompa. Swami Pranavananda spent much time at Trugo meditating and observing the Lake. On the western shore stands the Gossul gompa and on the north-western corner, the Chiu gompa. Five of these have now been partly revived with help from the government and the local people.

There are four chortens or stupas. Traditionally these contained a relic of the Buddha. They may also contain holy remains of lamas, inscriptions of the sacred mantra *Om Mani Padme Hum*, or any other sacred thing. Chortens are located at Langpona gompa in the north, and at Seralung, Trugo and Chiu.

There are four *chaktsal gangs* or places from where *sashtanga pranama,* or the prostration salute, is made. One is located on the eastern side just before Seralung gompa, two flank the Trugo gompa in the south and the fourth is on the north-western side at Tseti. Tibetans perform lengthy rituals at these places.

Towards Trugo

We are ready to take a break and have our porridge, but the stentorian woman who seems to lead the horsewallahs says we will stop a little later. She points to a vague undefined spot, and makes urgent rushed signals as though we must hurry through our walk. Some of our people refuse to budge, take off their clothes and make for the cool bosom of the Lake. The woman remains unmoved. She walks ahead with rapid steps till most of us feel compelled to follow.

After four and a half hours of walking, we find the caravan coming to a halt under the direction of our woman leader. We flop down and share our dry lunch – dates, nuts, *mathris*, *bhakhris*, biscuits and cheese. The Tibetans light a small fire with yak dung cakes. 'It is the main fuel of the country and burns almost smokeless with a hot, steady flame.'[1] A small pair of bellows is used to gather the scanty oxygen to get the flame aglow. On it goes the ubiquitous tea kettle; and they also carry *tsampa*, a powder made out of roasted barley. Preparing wholesome and hot food is not difficult for them. I try to take a photograph but they seem annoyed. Realizing it is shyness more than annoyance, I tell the old woman I want to take her pictures with me. She points to her missing teeth and the furrowed face. Using the Tibetan words for very good (*yagbodo* and *nying je po*), I tell her she is beautiful. She consents.

All along the way, the Tibetans wear fine gauze masks over their mouths and noses, much like those used in an operation theatre. When the wind blows, the fine sand around Manas embeds itself everywhere on the body. The masks help in keeping the nasal and oral passages clear of sand particles. As the eyes of the Tibetans are deep set and in the midst of a myriad wrinkles, they need no covering. Their skins are cracked and wizened due to continuous exposure to the clear and transparent light here; their faces look much older than they actually are, but their bodies display strong, sturdy movements. Our break is lengthy, seemingly unending. We begin to get restless because half the distance is still to be traversed.

Back on our way we encounter many swamps and streams, some quite deep and fast which cannot be forded on foot. The horses here are unlike the mules we used in India. They run away without notice and as their keepers give chase, the animals run faster still, overturning their load. The keepers go around nonchalantly, gathering the pieces and somehow getting the obdurate beasts to calm down and allow the bags to be replaced. The only solace is that they cannot get lost as the land is an open bowl and the horses, familiar with the

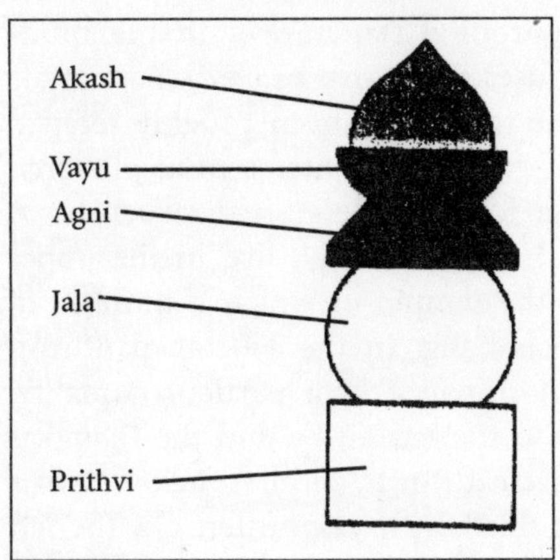

Elements associated with a Gompa.

route, will come back eventually. But the human cargo does suffer in the process. Panic causes some of us to slip off these unruly creatures more often than necessary. Sandeep, annoyed and disturbed that his horse sits down from time to time especially when fording streams, decides to walk all the way. He even wades through fast-moving, knee-deep waters that are icy cold. Persuasion does not change his mind.

We find that Tibetan horsewomen and men are peculiar; their choice of rider and horse does not make sense to us. Sandeep, the biggest man, is allocated the smallest horse and the animal insists on kneeling down when going through strong currents of water, while the wispy Bhairavi is made to sit on top of the biggest animal. As she hurls out complaints from that height, they insist she is perched atop the best animal and that no danger can befall her body.

It is almost 7 p.m. when we reach the Trugo monastery. The gompa is located where the water of the Lake is most calm and limpid and can be approached easily. From our rooms next to the shrine, we see the white dome of Kailash directly in front of our window, lovingly bathed in the light of the setting sun. Immediately in front, separating us and the mountain, stands the dark expanse of the Lake. I am exhausted, but wish to see what lies inside the temple adjacent to our newly-constructed rooms.

Passing a chorten covered with strings of prayer flags, and a row of *mani* stones, I reach the entrance. On the right side is a small windowless, low-roofed structure with the mud-plaster coming apart. It houses a massive prayer wheel made of brass. The murals on the walls have been roughly scraped off. Through a massive wooden door I enter a mud-plastered courtyard surrounded by a low double-storied structure. A lama and some others, perhaps his family, live in the upper sections. Straight ahead is the temple in which a number of fantastically painted thangkas hang. In the Tibetan pantheon every colour denotes the dominance of a particular quality. We are unable to understand the legend behind the thangkas due to the language barrier. In front is an altar, aglow with a row of innumerable lamps filled with yak butter. On the left is a long seat meant perhaps for the lamas who sit and chant mantras. At the end of this is the mandala, where Chinese yuans are piled. On the right is the solitary window which lets in an ethereal vision, the silvery dome of the mountain. Caught in this frame, it has a particularly uplifting influence on the mind.

Near the window is a large drum. I feel an impulse to lift the wooden sticks and experience the sound. The lama, together with his young assistant, immediately comes and prevents me from touching it. A little later Surendra comes in and resounds the drum. He is not denied the pleasure. I realize I have not seen any female lamas in the area.

The lama closes the large front doors after us. Then he beats the drum, a deep resonating sound that moves a current of heavy vibrations through the silence. This is the only sound acceptable in this abode of Shiva.

Coming back to our room we find a group of Tibetans filling it, there is no place for us even to stand. They stare at us unabashedly, with expressionless faces. It is not possible to know if they want anything, there is no response to our gesticulated queries. All efforts to make them leave bear no result. Instead, more men, women and children squeeze in wearing the traditional toga-like jackets. The room feels like an open market place. We cannot open our bags or freshen ourselves after the long day's march. Finally, the onset of darkness takes the Tibetans away, perhaps to the monastery.

Surendra and Tripathiji make tea while Durga and Kiran prepare the meal, cheese and noodles followed by some more tea. The kitchen is windowless and dark, but large enough to accommodate us all. Eating the food we cook ourselves after the day's walk is a pleasure we look forward to. A sense of communion and a sharing of experiences marks this time of the day.

The moon is now almost three-quarters full and sheds a clear cool light on the Lake. It is a wondrous crystallization of a scene I had created in my mind's eye and longed to actually see. I slip out when all is quiet. The Lake is a sheet of silver at the base of the mountain and the sky above a silent expanse of stars and moonlight. Never before had I seen a sky so brilliant in the middle of the night. Not a single cloud obstructs the sight. The waters, as if in reciprocation to the heavens above, renounce their ripples and merge in the silence. The mountains stand like phantom spectators. Nothing moves.

Like the Lake, the mind stills itself in response to the surroundings. There is no thought, stillness is all that is experienced; no reaction, just absorption. Void merging into void. This is how the universe must have been before creation – pregnant with the possibility of experience, itself without any.

Where Nothing is Predictable

> . . . now calm, serene, and silent even like the space beyond, and now disturbed raising tempestuous winds flinging even the sheep and goats in the surroundings; now a beautiful blue and now a hard white mass, Lake Manasarovar, with her hundreds of avatars and myriads of changing forms, offers an engima to the puny self-conceited human being to think, meditate, and perhaps ultimately fail to comprehend all these. All hail, Oh Manas !! Lake of the Royal Sages and Swans!! Victory to Thee!!
>
> Swami Pranavananda
>
> *Kailash Manasarovar*

We have a journey of 32 kilometres ahead of us today. We start off on time because the horses and their keepers are lodged where we are. The body has lost its active predisposition and surrendered itself to the momentum of the journey. We move on like automatons propelled by a self-generated energy.

I have decided to walk the whole distance, even across the fast-moving icy rivulets. The Lake has by now, become an extension of the mind which bathes and merges in it, striving to cleanse itself of the alchemy of thought. It wants to be like the sky, reflected in the Lake without the mass of clouding mists. The beauty of the Lake and mountains, the lightness of the air create a meditative frame of mind.

The horsewallahs are more friendly than before. They empathize with our anxieties and limitations, but the decisions about stopping and moving are still theirs. Going past the chorten we walk through a ground cover of tiny blue flowers that look like miniature cornflowers. A little subterranean water is enough to set this virgin soil abloom. We are now headed westward along the southern shore of the sacred waters. The sun rises behind us. Everything – the weather, the wind, the soil – feels surreal. While the sun scorches the head, forcing us to wear our wide-brimmed hats, the rest of the body feels cold. The wind from the Lake is icy though the sun is hotter than we have known it in the plains. Different parts of the body have to be treated differently as though they were individual, autonomous entities. Quicksilver changes of weather mark the area.

Soon after leaving, we see a pitch-black cloud rising on our left. If it overtakes us we are bound to be soaked to the skin. But after a walk of just two hours, our guides decide to stop for food. Today we are not hungry, but they are adamant; some of us walk on anyway. I watch the Tibetans preparing food. They carry a bag full of flat, round bread with a hole in the centre. They offer me some. It is tasty, something like a fried chapati. They eat it with their tea, prepared as usual without much ado. They offer me some more bread. The old woman says it is called *rota.* Through sign language she establishes that it is made from rice flour, or so I understand. There is much laughter and jollity at my questions. The man who had a rift with Sandeep earlier for not holding his horse offers me a cigarette. I refuse. He insists. Perhaps he thinks I am shy. He forces one on me. After a difficult and somewhat lengthy vocal joust, I manage to return his gift. Is he disappointed? Maybe I should have taken a puff before giving it back to him.

It appears that our guide-companions want a long break. So I also decide to move on. The sun is now above our heads, the Lake still. We look back and sight the monastery we left three hours ago, a white sheet of snow has fallen on it. There are no clouds there. The clouds actually appear to be coming from a different direction. Hence the Hindi saying: *Manasarovar kaun pharse, bin badal him barse*: 'Who can assess the Manasarovar, for snow falls here in the absence of clouds.' Heinrich Harrer, in the preface of his book, *Return to Tibet,* says that here one does not have to invent or think of miracles. There is enough that is extraordinary and nothing happens in a predictable fashion. As far as the weather is concerned, even Tibetans are unable to make any judgement whatsoever. Experience has taught them to admit that they do not know.

The clouds continue to move rapidly but their direction is elusive. At some distance behind us we can see a dark mass of rain. It must be further away than we think. We hear the distant collision of clouds. The Lake begins to look dark. Strong waves rise and edge the shore leaving white foam as they recede. It looks more like an ocean. That which had looked serene and tranquil not so long ago is now releasing its latent energy in response to the sky above. The clear reflection of Kailash is now lost in its turbulent depths.

> Like the mind, the Manasarovar is all-encompassing and capable of infinite moods, and the endless dissolution and recreation of thoughts is mirrored by the clouds which rise from the lake's depths, only to water them again with rain.
>
> Kerry Moran
>
> *The Sacred Mountain of Tibet*

The walk is unending. The unobstructed landmarks scattered through the vast landscape delude rather than aid judgement with regard to distance. Soon after we turn the rounded south-western bend to walk along the western shore of the Lake, we witness an enchanting sight. The clouds have lifted and the Gossul gompa stands in front, a massive projection on top of a sheer rock promontory. Its plinth is at least 200 feet above our heads. The gompa can only be approached from the other side which is away from the Lake. Had we been a little further away from the Lake, skirting the small hill on its shore, we could have entered it. The gompa is located at a place where the waters are exceptionally clear, and the monastery must command a magnificent view of the Lake in its entirety against a backdrop of the mountain shrine. Atisha Srijnana, the great Indian scholar and monk, is said to have stayed in a cave in the massive rock in A.D. 1042 when he was on his way to the monastery of Tholing at Tsaparang, further west. Gossul gompa did not exist then. The mind boggles to think how anyone would have thought of building here and living in these desolate surroundings, immersing the mind in nothing but the vacuity of space. A solitary dwelling, it is open only to the skies above and the water ahead. The structure appears to form a part of the sheer rock face of the mountain. Who would have brought all the material here to build this massive structure?

We can see the horses, small specks coming up in the distance. Despite the emptiness it is not easy to spot things because of the peculiar quality of the light, and the great distances. Ahead of us we see a small dot – it is the building in which we are to stay the night; we do not mislead ourselves by harbouring hopes of reaching it soon. Now the Lake is a sheet of shimmering metallic silver, hard to look at. It has been changing colour every half hour; its force and power seem to reside in its capacity to remain intact as a Lake, even as it receives all that is around. It creates and recreates ceaselessly. As Shakti, even when it remains in inseparable union with Shiva, the nonchanging ever-present being, there is no belonging, only Being, as neither possesses the other.

It is more than eight hours since we started walking. The leader tries to persuade me to sit on the horse. But I am going to walk today. The waters are lapping at the heart, washing away the burden of memories, of hopes and dejections, of loves and betrayals, of aspirations and non-fulfilment. The intermingling of mind with the Mind is calming. The heart experiences only a flow and an enveloping, as though an inner core made of love had found an opening. I experience a strange tiredness and decide to stretch out flat on my back beside the Lake, my face raised to the brightness of the firmament above.

Of Monks and Sacred Spaces

When mind has no place where it can stop, and become limited, the Mahamudra, the Great Attitude, is present. By cultivating such an attitude one attains supreme enlightenment.

Tilopa, the great-grand guru of Milarepa

Acharya Deepankar Srijnana (popularly known as Atisha), a scholar at the Vikramshila university in India, spent one week in a cave carved out in the rock which is now the site for Gossul gompa. Atisha was an Indian monk of royal birth. Born in A.D. 980 to King Kalyan Sri of Bengal, Atisha displayed signs of greatness from childhood. Renouncing his right to wealth and kingship like the Buddha, he went in search of spiritual teachers and gurus in Nalanda and Suvarnadip. He also gained directions from his tutelary deity, Tara. Due to his great scholarship, he rose to become the rector of the Vikramshila University. He went to Tibet in A.D. 1038 at the age of 58, and died in A.D. 1052 at the age of 72, near Lhasa. He is greatly revered by the Tibetans for his wisdom and is regarded as an incarnation of Manjusri Bodhisattva. Among other achievements, he is credited with purifying Buddhism of certain lowly tendencies, and for restoring the Mahayana doctrine to its pristine purity.[1]

Atisha had been invited to Tibet by the monk-King La Lhama (also known by the name of Yeshe O). It was a period of uncertainty for Buddhism in Tibet; the faith had suffered a setback at the hands of the followers of Bon, the indigenous religion of Tibet. There was conflict even among those who professed to follow Buddhism – the followers of the Vinaya School and those who followed the Tantric School. A number of Indians travelled to Tibet during this period. But their search was for gold; they pretended to have great knowledge of Tantra and cheated the Tibetans by 'behaving truculently and employing black arts.'[2] This saddened King Lha Lama greatly. In this context, the arrival of Atisha via Kailash and Manasarovar was a high point of the Buddhist renaissance in Tibet.

Buddhism initially made its way into Tibet during the earlier half of the seventh century in the reign of King Songtsen Gampo (meaning Songtsen, the Most Accomplished). His Chinese and Nepalese wives, Wencheng and Trhisun, were ardent followers of Buddhism and instrumental in influencing the King into propagating the doctrine. The King sent Thonmi Sambhota together with sixteen others to Kashmir to study the art of writing so that Buddhist texts could be rendered into the Tibetan language. While most of them perished because they were unable to bear the heat of the Indian climate, Sambhota returned and created a Tibetan alphabet based on the Sanskrit characters of the time. This made possible the translation of several books into Tibetan.[3]

After Songtsen Gampo, another king who worked for the spread of Buddhism was Trhisong Detsen. He invited two well-known Indian teachers, Santarakshita and Padmasambhava to Tibet. Santarakshita was the head of the

Buddhist University of Nalanda. Faced with difficulties from the local shamanistic religion in Tibet, he advised the king to invite another teacher, Padmasambhava from India. Padmasambhava was a powerful exorcist and could counter the onslaught of the Bon priests. The two built the famous monastery of Samye near Lhasa. The model of the monastery was based on that of Odantapuri in Bengal. It is said to have contained the forms of Sumeru and twelve continents. King Detsen died in A.D. 797.

The third great religious king Ralpachan was assassinated in A.D. 838. His older brother, Langdarma, who succeeded him was an avowed adherent of the Bon religion. After the death of Langdarma in A.D. 842, the ruling dynasty of central Tibet disintegrated and Buddhism, too, was rooted out.[4]

Nevertheless, descendants of the royal dynasty moved away and established small kingdoms in western Tibet. Two of these, La Lhama (or Yeshe O) and his grandnephew Changchup O, were monk-kings. Legend has it that Lha Lama, King of Mnahri, sent many Tibetan scholars to India to learn Sanskrit and translate Buddhist sutras into Tibetan. Many died and one of the few who returned was Rinchen Sangpo, the great translator. Finally, the King started collecting gold with the purpose of inviting Indian scholars to Tibet so that they could preach the unsullied doctrine. A messenger was sent to invite Atisha. Atisha declined the invitation because he had much work to do. La Lhama presumed that Atisha had refused because the quantity of gold sent was not enough. So he started out on an expedition to the north to collect more gold. This worried the king of Garlog; if La Lhama was not stopped, Buddhism would once again gain ground in Tibet. The king of Garlog captured and imprisoned Lha Lama. Changchup O (or Jang-chub-Hod), Lha Lama's nephew, went to seek his uncle's release but the king said he wanted gold equal to the weight of the prisoner to set him free. On receiving it he still refused, and asked for more gold, equal to the weight of his head. Lha Lama smiled at this and told his nephew that his body was old and not worth so much trouble.

'Do not give even one coin to the Garlog king. Take all the gold to India to invite Atisha and deliver this message to the Pandita. For you and the sake of our religion I have sacrificed my life to the Garlog King. My great longing is to spread Buddhism in Tibet. Therefore, please fulfil this desire and I shall pray for blessings to fall upon you in future lives.'

This tale of the king's sacrifice deeply moved Atisha who felt compelled to go to Tibet. Even so, it took him 18 months to complete the work at hand before he could leave India. Before departing for Tibet he made a pilgrimage to Bodh Gaya, where his tutelary deity Tara told him he would lose 20 years of his life by travelling to Tibet. In India he would live to be 92 whereas in Tibet he would die at 72. Yet, the work of his life was to be performed in Tibet and that he should go. Unperturbed, Atisha decided to go. He donated the gold brought for him to the Vikramshila University.

On his way, Atisha spent a year in Nepal preaching the doctrine; he also stayed at Khojarnath during the monsoons. He then passed Lake Manasarovar on his way to the kingdom of Guge in western Tibet, where his work was waiting for him. He is said to have spent a total of nine months in the Kailash Manasarovar region engaging himself in varied spiritual practices. Atisha's skeleton and drinking bowl are believed to have been preserved in a monastery at Kailash.

Atisha attracted the devotion and attention of even ordinary people in Tibet, as he gave due respect to the tantric and magical practices that were present in local religions. Instead of denying or deriding them, he incorporated them into the Buddhist doctrine. He also mastered the Tibetan language, a feat difficult for an Indian teacher. Atisha was inclined to propagate spiritual discipline for the benefit of his fellow beings, rather than indulge in magical practices or scholarship. When he reached western Tibet, he was received with respect. But the old venerated translator Rinchen Sangpo, now eighty-two years old, refused to show respect to Atisha initially. But when he listened to Atisha expounding the Madhyamika philosophy, his understanding of spiritual wisdom widened. Seeing that the translator wished to practise religion righteously, Atisha exhorted him to not let his mind wander into evil. He is supposed to have said to Rinchen Sangpo, 'O Great Translator! The sufferings of the phenomenal world are difficult to bear. One should labour for the benefit of all living beings. Now, pray practise meditation!'[5] It is believed that after Atisha's departure from western Tibet, Rinchen Sangpo practised one-pointed meditation for ten years and reached the highest realization.

Three years had passed and it was time for Atisha's return to Vikramshila; he had promised so, to the authorities at the University. But during his return journey, at the Lipu Pass, his tutelary deity informed him that he was yet to find his chief disciple in Tibet for whose sake he had to stay longer. It was then that he found 'Brom-ston', his main disciple who spread the doctrine after him. Atisha was the founder of the Ka-dam-pa order in Tibet,[6] from which the new Ka-dam-pa or Yellow Hat order is derived. At Tholing in western Tibet, he wrote the *Bodhipathapradipa*, or Lamp for the Way of Enlightenment. Atisha brought a uniformity in the Buddhist teachings in Tibet which before him were fragmentary. He established that all the teachings of the Buddha were for the deliverance of the individual in various stages, to Nirvana.

In the period between the tenth and the twelfth centuries, tremendous activity took place in Tibet. Innumerable Tibetans went to India and many preachers came from India; they translated not only the original texts but all the commentaries and connected texts into Tibetan. It is recognized that whole generations of trained Tibetan translators were so consistent in their translations of Sanskrit Buddhist texts that later generations of teachers and students (who neither knew Sanskrit nor had ever been to India) could overlook the fact that the books they studied were foreign in origin. By the twelfth century, a skilled minority of Tibetans had transferred to Tibetan soil not only the texts but the whole way of life of Indian Buddhist monks and yogins.[7]

As a result, there was no dismay in Tibet over the disappearance of Buddhism in its land of origin. Buddhism, which had connected Tibet to countries outside its borders, later became the factor for its isolation after the twelfth century. 'Buddhism which had once been practised by all of Tibet's neighbours . . . was now practised by the Tibetans alone.'[8] The religion had lost most of its adherents in the land of its origin and the great universities nurtured by Buddhist scholars in India had been destroyed by invaders from abroad.

The result of this hectic and focused activity to spread Buddhism in Tibet was that when the original texts in India were destroyed, it was in Tibet that they could be found in translated form. It is said that even now, the number of translated texts is so great that just cataloguing them would take several years.

Chaktsal Gang at Tseti

Finally, our resting place is within reach. Tseti on the western side of the waters is sacred to Hindu pilgrims. Part of the ashes of Mahatama Gandhi's body are said to have been immersed here. We had our first *darshan* of the holy Lake from here when we set out from Taklakot for the base of Kailash. From the beginning to the end, we have completed one circuit of the lake. A number of flag poles adorn the shores. This is one of the Chaktsal gangs, a place for full-body prostration for the Tibetans. Hindus like to take a ritual bath here; the water is calm. Tibetans, while they visit and camp on the open sands around it, do not bathe in it as they believe that will pollute the water. They take the water in their hands and pour it on their foreheads, but for the Hindus immersing themselves in it is an important ritual.

Our rooms are a welcome relief after the seemingly interminable walk. There are two rooms adjacent to each other with four beds along each wall. The four women get the windowless room with no direct outlet to the open courtyard. A third room is located slightly away. Inside our room I feel a sense of suffocation after the exertion at this altitude. Despite homeopathic medicines and the consumption of plenty of liquids, the feeling of asphyxiation does not go away. While the body wants rest, the mind does not wish to be away from the holy sight. I scrub my body with cleansing towelettes hoping to feel better.

Tea is served by the young stalwarts who always reach earlier and have become accustomed to lighting the stove. The keeper of this guesthouse is a surly man with thick-set features. The lively Tibetan horse-women come in, making fun of and chorusing the two phrases of Tibetan I had used most freely in an attempt to make them slow down or wait for us before fording a stream. *Nguroh Nang, Ngruho Nang, Tu je chhe*, they scream in unison as they double up in a fit of giggles. They have come to bid farewell. Perhaps they will accompany the other half of our group which arrives a day later. They will probably hitch a ride on a truck to go back to their village at Houre. Or they may walk back today along with their animals, through the rough section of the part which we covered by bus.

As we come out for tea, we notice a sudden convergence of Tibetans and their tents along the shore of the lake. In two days it will be *purnima,* the full-moon night, an auspicious time to perform the Kailash parikrama. Like us the Tibetans will complete their round of the Lake before moving on to the base of the mountain. I watch a man and a woman under a flag-studded pole which forms a sort of canopy over them. They perform a series of *sashtang namaskars* facing the Mountain across the Lake. They continuously chant mantras and repeat strenuous physical movements – going down flat on their bellies so that all parts of the body may touch the earth. I had noticed them earlier and now, an hour later, they are still fully absorbed in their *sadhana*. As it is not taboo to stand and stare, I do. Occasionally, the man glances at me from the corner of his eyes. Soon, another man emerges from a tent, lights a lamp, and begins to chant mantras. He has a decanter of a brew that looks like tea. At intervals, he pours a bit of the brew into a small ceramic bowl and drains it out towards the lake. As he faces north, where the mountain is, the Lake is to his right. I sit near him in an attempt to record his voice. He does not mind. In fact he puts on the demeanour of a performer for an appreciative audience. Generally, Tibetans seem unperturbed by cameras or recorders. Like the Lake they accept everything as it comes and goes.

A little later, I walk up the hill beside the camp. Surendra and Desai are already sitting at the top, waiting for a clear view of the sacred mountain. Somehow, without the reflection of the mountain in the Lake, the picture is not quite complete. Today, the mountain has been hiding behind clouds; we sit for a long time. We have no desire to go away until the clouds have lifted but there is no sign of that happening. The sun is about to set and the air is becoming chilly. We continue to sit as though beseeching the deity to uncover itself. Then suddenly, I get a startling glimpse of the south face looking down silently, benignly, from above a thin veil of mist. My heart pounds as it comes face to face with the deeply longed for presence. There is benediction in the air. A desire to kneel down and prostrate takes over. Inwardly assured of the deity's acknowledgement, we walk back to the camp.

This camp right beside the lake is particularly short of water. The keeper who brings bucketsfull from the lake is not keen to make unnecessary trips, and he prevents us from using water even to wash the dishes. He is annoyed because we have not yet cooked, so absorbed were we in the *satsanga* on the shores of the lake after a successful completion of the *parikrama*.

The sky is bright with stars and the moonlight now seems to penetrate the farthest reaches of the firmament. Soon Durga comes out saying that the keeper has locked the kitchen and gone to sleep. He refuses to let us do any cooking. It takes much persuasion and the intervention of his kindly wife; we had earlier presented her with a pair of large earrings from India. He comes out grumpily to open the door. We assure him that we will light the stove ourselves and lock the door when we are done, and that he could go back to sleep. But he insists on sitting with us right through. We hurriedly make soup and noodles, take the food out of the kitchen and allow him to lock up.

At night, the feeling of suffocation takes over again to bring up the creeping doubt: 'Will I make it?' Gasping, I go out quietly for some deep breaths. In the distance the white tents glow like luminous structures. Some torchlights move about busily. The Tibetan pilgrims have created a veritable township. The Lake is ripple free alongside the phantom movement of these religious people. They do not disturb the silence. Have these devout beings not slept at all? I watch for a while before going in. After a short sleep I come out again less than two hours later; the sky is lighter and there is no sign of the township. They probably started out with the first ray of light to complete their journey to Kailash or get back to their homes in distant places.

Today is our day of rest. We are not bound by the regimen of movement and of reaching a given place before nightfall. With nothing specific to do after the continuous journey, there is a sense of freedom. Breathing is still difficult, but the light of the day has a way of reducing the impact of bodily afflictions. I do not wish to think too much about it. We go for a bath in the Lake – my first in the freezing water. Some of our people have been bathing every day since we came. As I gingerly immerse half my body, my breath feels held up in the upper part of the chest and I find it difficult to dip the head, an essential for ritual cleansing. It will have to remain my 'Achilles heel'. We wash our clothes in the holy waters and dry them on the stones, trying to avoid the defiling remains of the Tibetans who do not mind leaving their excrement on the shores, much of which will be washed into the lake by the waves. Since it is impossible to find a large enough rock to squat behind, Tibetans fulfil bodily necessities out in the open, without undue fuss about privacy. This is a land of stripping to the core. No formal barriers separate humans from their surroundings.

Kiran prepares some halwa for the *havan* we are going to perform on the banks of the *Shakti peeth*, where the energy of the Devi in her living form is supposed to reside. Others put together incense, *prasad*, twigs for the fire. As advised, we perform the ritual before eleven in the morning. As soon as we finish a strong piercing gale begins to blow, making it impossible for us to stay outdoors. The rest of the day is spent resting and ruminating.

Chiu Gompa

Garry is to come at 11 a.m. to take us to Dharchen so that we may swap places with the other group left at the base of Kailash. Many of our group are interested in seeing the Chiu Gompa on the way, about six kilometres from our camp. While at Tseti, we did not have enough strength to walk there, even though we had a free day. Garry agrees to our request on the condition that we do not tell anyone – not even Dorje, his partner in planning and guiding these trips. Whatever his reasons for eliciting this promise, we agree readily.

A twenty-minute drive brings us to this very sacred gompa where the Boddhisattva is said to have left his body. There are a couple of large and ornate chortens and numerous cairns of well-carved Mani stones bedecked with flags and yak horns. The cairns are so large and conical that they look like chortens themselves. A tunnel of narrow steps takes us up and around the monastery. We reach a small dark room, and proceed over rough, uneven steps into the inner sanctum. For a moment we stand spellbound in the warm glow of the innumerable butter lamps, and the beautiful mandala altar on which offerings are made. Outside in the landing, a window provides a breathtaking view of the Lake – an unending expanse of turquoise-blue tranquility. On a bench are hundreds of rectangular blocks of butter meant for the lamps on the altar. The lama here does not allow any photographs to be taken. I give him some of the pills consecrated by the Dalai Lama at a special ceremony held at Bodh Gaya. It takes a while for him to understand, for in Tibet the Divine Ruler is referred to as *Gyalwa Rinpoche* (the Victorious One) or *Kyapgon Rinpoche* (Precious Protector). The title 'Dalai Lama', was conferred on Sonam Gyatso in 1579 when he was invited to Mongolia. The word in Mongolian, *Ta le* (now written as Dalai) stands for 'a priest with ocean-like wisdom'.[9] Once he understands, the lama at Chiu immediately allows many of us to use our flashes.

Chiu, the 'bird-gompa', is perched high on a rock. Several streamers of prayer flags flutter in the breeze as they flow down from the chortens and the amazing height of the monastery. The view from above is expansive. It is impossible to live in this vast solitude and not commune with the silent deep. Perhaps it is silent communion and not movement in space that provides knowledge of the underlying energy. Here, it seems possible to be in touch with the reality which is the substance, the substratum of creation.

The rooms of the lamas are at the back, built into the mountain wall, while the prayer areas are located on the projection hanging out over the Lake. Once again I am amazed by the adventurous souls who built these massive, isolated structures.

The Lake here is silent, taking the surroundings into its deep clarity. Kailash resides within it, undistorted, merged in the limpid waters, invisible to the onlooker. There is no identity, no history here, only the present and an unquestioning, total surrender. There is no conflict, no resistance, only existence and beingness – a shedding of the personality.

At the Foot of Kailash

We take the same route that we followed earlier, to go to Dharchen at the base of Kailash, past Ganga Chhu. A continuous stream of pilgrims, in trucks and on foot, traverse the Barkha plain. They display no consciousness of discomfort in their journey. Excitement alone is writ large on their faces. As we approach Dharchen, we can see hordes of sheep and long-horned goats that yield the precious wool which once made Tibetans rich. It may be because of these goats that Lhasa, or the land of the Gods, was earlier known as Rasa, the land of the goats, before Buddhism made its way into Tibet![10] There are yaks and horses too. All these belong to the nomads who travel long distances defying the weather and the rough terrain.

At Dharchen, we meet the other half of our group and exchange notes and tips. Soon they are on their way to Manas to perform the yatra we have just completed. It is *purnima* today, an auspicious day for the performance of the circumambulation. There are many more tents today than when we first came. The Tibetans perform the *parikrama* in one day, walking day and night. This saves them the trouble of carrying too many provisions and the expense of staying overnight.

I make my acquaintance with Li, the Chinese guide we had met briefly while at Taklakot. He will be our guide and interpreter around Kailash because Dorje, the official guide who knows Kailash well does not perform this task himself these days. I try hard to persuade Dorje to accompany us but very politely and skilfully, smiling through golden teeth, he convinces us that he cannot. He has to look after a number of pilgrims from all over the world, and he has relatives visiting him. His spirit will be with us at every step, he says. He will provide all the information we want when we get back, and ensure that we get the best yaks and yak men. His politeness is disarming; we have to agree.

On a visit to his home in the afternoon, we meet his sister (a resident of Bihar who has temporarily shifted to Nepal) and her husband, and some other relatives. There are also pilgrims who have come from great distances, all drinking unceasing rounds of black tea poured out even before the glasses are half empty.

Dorje says that the lama sitting in his room can predict people's future. Many people there ask questions which are generally answered in a single sentence in Tibetan. They offer him *khattas* (cotton gauze scarves which are a token of respect) and some money, together with gifts. Dorje says I can also ask him something if I wish when there are not so many people around.

A little later, I am in Dorje's room again. The lama wants a question to be asked before he will predict anything. The only question that surfaces in the mind is why I undertook this journey. He says a dark spectre was haunting me, the spectre of death. It was constantly in my way in the recent past, but now that I have been called to do the Kailash *parikrama* it will be taken care of. The disturbance in the mind, the obstacles along the path, will all be cleared. It takes quite a few minutes for this prophecy to be worked out as it has to be translated and relayed in a triangular fashion. I feel that I lose something in the process. If only I knew the language, the interaction could have been richer.

Back in our room, I renew interaction with Li on whose cooperation much of the success of this consequential part of the yatra depends. He is a delicately-built, aristocratic-looking Chinese, about twenty-three. He took the job here (more than 3,000 kilometres from his hometown of Nanjing), because he was told he could earn good money, and that the scenery was beautiful. So he joined the Tourist Company of Ali. The money is not much, only 240 yuans per month. Even though it is a good amount by Chinese standards, there are others in his family who make more back home without having to go through the rigours of such a journey. To get here, he had to travel to Shi Quan-He, Kashgar and Urumqi and then by truck for a few hundred kilometres. Still, he likes it because the scenery is indeed spectacular, and he gets a chance to meet different kinds of people. He is not sure if he will come back next year. The return journey by train from Urumqi will cost 200 yuan, but he feels good that he can now pay for himself without having to rely on his parents. This was why he took the job. He has a girl-friend in Nanjing; she studies English and her father teaches Hindi at the University. He will learn Hindi before he comes to India, he says.

I become fond of this elegant young man with the hands of a dancer. He was learning ballet till his parents dissuaded him from taking it up as a profession; there is not much money in it. So he started learning English. His mother is an English teacher, but he learnt from another teacher as well and got this job.

'Tourist Company of Ali' is a strange name for a company in Tibet. The actual word is Ngari, Dorje explains. The syllable '*Ng*' is a Tibetan letter which cannot be pronounced by the Chinese. So it becomes 'a' and since 'r' is often interchanged with 'l' in Chinese, '*Ngari*' becomes Ali.

As I talk to Li, a beautiful lilting sound emerges from the room behind us. One of the Tibetan girls is singing, and I want to record her song. She is extremely shy and giggles hysterically. Her companion tries to persuade her, but she too is caught by a fit of giggles. Li cajoles the singer, and to prevent the other from distracting her, he holds her down – one hand tightly cupped on her mouth. It is almost a wrestling match. Finally, we get a few minutes of song on tape – a Tibetan folk song, sung in the original and in Chinese. Every Tibetan song seems to have a Chinese version. The song and the voice have a haunting melody – about a person who longs for home as he travels in distant lands. He wishes he were free as a bird and could fly back to where he came from. I play back the song. The girl looks happy and surprised, perhaps this is the first time she has heard her own voice being played back.

Dharchen is well provided with basic amenities. It has a telephone connection with Taklakot from where our welfare is relayed to India. There is electricity for longer hours here. But there is no water, least of all for bathing. We rearrange our bags and sort out the things we need for the three days of Kailash *parikrama*. Food has to be replenished. Sugar has run short, so we buy a kilo for ten yuans when foodstuff is actually far cheaper here. Black marketing is not far below the surface, even here.

In the evening Dorje comes and spends time with us. He narrates stories about Kailash, the gompas around it, about Milarepa, the great Tibetan sage, and Atisha. He talks about his own efforts at preserving Tibetan culture; Kailash and the Buddha are the two most important symbols for the Tibetans. Dorje was born here and lives at Dharchen, summer or winter. His Hindi is perfect because of his education in Banaras. He visits India quite regularly as he has family there, but more than that the attraction of the Dalai Lama takes him there. He represents the cause of the Tibetan identity in every forum and will continue to do so, he says.

He is much impressed by our feeling and devotion for Kailash. He would have liked to take us to Tirthapuri and Guge Kingdom; but it is too late to arrange this now because it requires prior permission. These two places should be included in the plan for the following groups, he says. We assure him that we will suggest it to the organizers in India.

Through the Gateway of Death

Those who follow Shiva tread strange paths and see strange visions. Shiva is a divine thriller. The path to Shiva is a mountain ride that jolts the seeker, pitching him into high altitude conditions that leave him breathless with the euphoria of dread.

Shiva batters his devotee, blows his mind and boggles his imagination. Scaling the heights of Kailash, the sights and sounds that greet him are not calculated to soothe. The seeker needs to brace himself to hear the sounds, as he needs to steel himself for the first vision of Shiva . . .

Adapted from Lakshmi Lal's
Eye of the Storm: Shiva

We leave Dharchen at 9.45 Beijing time. As usual, the sky above does not tally with the time observed here. But then time too, is a construct of the human mind.

Dorje had emphasized that everyone must first walk up to a meadow about five kilometres away, and from there those who wish to ride yaks can do so. At the beginning of the narrow passage through the scrub, Dorje oversees our departure. He mumbles some mantras for the successful completion of our journey and seems to bless us. The path is uneven and riven with gashes in the ground. The effects of deep subterranean activity are visible here. Deep fissures reflect the harsh conditions the earth has lived through, and the changes it will continue to be subjected to. Like in the human body, here too, energy releases itself through the most sensitive points in the structure. It is the fragile junction of the neck which conducts the energy from the lower chakras to the more subtle centres of knowledge and wisdom in the head. It is also at the sensitive throat level that sound, which remains an undifferentiated mass lower down, turns into the fiery energy of speech.

Down below is a valley with a stream opening out into it. It will be dangerous to ride through this place. I walk with Li and Bhairavi. It is tough for her to walk even this distance. She trudges along, clad in a long plastic raincoat that flaps around her small body – 'from USA', she proclaims.

The altitude tires us soon. After an hour the yak men arrive – some yaks loaded with our bags and others, free. Li prevails upon them to take Bhairavi. They are cooperative because they can handle one light-weight rider through the steep inclines. This makes progress easier. Two hours later we reach the open meadow where the others are waiting. They had been instructed not to proceed further till all of the group are assembled. Unlike the Manas *parikrama*, it is possible to lose one's way here, and in the mountain ranges the search is not easy. Also, unlike the Manas *parikrama*, the terrain is uneven, calling for greater effort.

The meadow is at a place called Proclamation Pass, and it is a Chaktsal Gang. The *parikrama* formally begins from here, and the first view of Kailash can be had on a clear day. At the northern side of the meadow stands a chorten and a large pole with thousands of brightly-coloured flags strung on it, a massive canopy. Every year in May there is a big ceremony when thousands of visitors gather to bring down the pole, put up fresh prayer flags and then re-erect the pole. It is a major ritual involving a large number of people due to the sheer size of the pole. Three months ago, this being the year of the iron-horse, many more than the usual number of visitors came.

Li demonstrates the correct method of riding a yak. Yaks do not have a bridle, only a string goes around the neck; so one must sit behind the wooden saddle meant to carry loads, and cling on for dear life. To get off, one must slide down the back. Despite our fears, we find the yak gentler than the mule. With its short legs and large body, it does not walk very fast and manoeuvres the slopes nimbly. It is sensitive enough not to push people walking alongside; it moves up or down the slope as it passes by them. Dorje had jokingly asked me to tell my co-yatris that riding on the back of a yak is like riding on Nandi, the bull of Shiva. He himself never rides one. 'Despite this,' he said, 'people will ride yaks, but you must tell them anyway.' His emphatic statement makes me decide not to try. Besides, Li has reassured me, 'You can do it walking ma'am, I will always be with you.'

After a short break and some refreshments we move on. Six of us are determined to walk all the way. We decide to meet at the next meadow two hours later. Li explains the route, and with maps provided by Garry there is no chance of going astray. We walk along the western side of Kailash through a narrow canyon between what look like megalithic sandstone mountains. With slate, rubble, sandstone and granite, Kailash presents different facets from different points.

On our left, on a mountain to the west of Kailash, stands the Chukku monastery. It seems to hang far up in a cliff on the mountain. It is only after some concentration that I am able to see the narrow winding steps dug into the mountain face up to the monastery, more than a thousand feet above us. Like the other monasteries around Kailash this too has its particular history. It was inhabited by a woman who gained extraordinary powers due to rigorous practices and began to look upon herself as special. It was with difficulty that she was driven out of here by a more powerful lama.

Milarepa is said to have shown the way to go around Kailash by the flight of a black crow. He followed the path and came to certain caves along the way which, over the years, were turned into monasteries. Of the six Kailash monasteries, apparently this is the first to have been rebuilt after the Cultural Revolution. It is reputed to house a statue of Chukku Rinpoche, the founder of the monastery. His statue is said to be the source of many miracles.

It is believed that the gompa also had a conch-shell with a silver lining, brought from Lake Manasarovar through a miracle. There was also a copper vessel brought from India by the Buddhist monk Tilopa who was the guru of Milarepa. Together, the three objects were taken to represent the Buddha's body, speech and mind.

At the beginning of the path is an arch-like construction called *yama dvar,* the gateway of death. This death is symbolic, as dying to one's personality is necessary before renewal can be achieved. Dying implies the shedding of impure layers that cover the luminous purity within. 'Do not cling to that which you have known yourself to be,' the entrance to Kailash seems to say. We walk through a narrow opening between massive sandstone mountains. Due to the red colour of the rocks, this area is known as the valley of Amitabha Buddha, the Buddha of the Rising Sun.

On a clear day, the icy dome of Kailash appears above the rock pillars and the cornices. It is covered by clouds today and yet, it uncovers itself just a little to provide a view of the face carved into the linga – a mingling of the physical and the abstract symbols. From here it is often possible to see distinctly the three eyes of Shiva: they appear embedded in the massive symbol. The right and the left eyes stand for the sun, the principle of heat; and for the moon, the principle of coolness. Metaphysically speaking, they stand for the higher (*vigyana*) and the lower mind (*pragyana*). The latter is not constant like the former.[1] The third vertical eye, distinctive to

Shiva, represents fire – a balance between the two principles necessary for creation as well as sustenance. It can be said to represent the 'state of absolute unity' which, paradoxically, is 'the ultimate source of all creation'.[2]

The three eyes are also symbolic of 'the trinitarian principle of manifestation. They correspond to the three cities: the city of gold which is Heaven; the city of silver which is the Intermediate region; and the city of copper which is the Earth. These three cities are destructive when they are discreet, but it is the great power of Shiva which pierces them with his single shaft and keeps them together, or integrated in their functioning.'[3] Kailash stands as a shaft connecting the earth with heaven, as it pierces through the firmament.

The third eye is both auspicious and destructive. It reduces untruth and impurity into ashes while blessing that which is bereft of ego, the sense of doership. This eye turned Kamadeva, the god of love, to ashes when he tried to disturb the *tapas* of Shiva. But it opened to witness the wedding of Rama, a symbol of the Higher Mind. This seeing was one of benediction.[4]

The linga is also reflective of Shiva's temporal transcendence. The *Linga Purana* states that when the column of fire appeared before Brahma and Vishnu, 'the sound AUM rang loudly from the flame linga'.[5] The two gods, Brahma and Vishnu, were debating which of the two was greater. At this point the column manifested itself, and neither of the gods could find its beginning or end – thereby revealing that greatness lies beyond. AUM, the eternal, ever-existent syllable, is *beyond.* It also represents the three facets of time – past, present and future.

This, the western face of the mountain, shows us one of the four visible faces of Shiva. The god himself explained to his consort Uma or Parvati, the import of these four faces, telling her that 'the eastern face conveyed the supernatural and the perennial practice of asceticism, the western face expressed the sustenance of the universe, and the northern face showed meditation on the Veda, the sum total of all knowledge. The northern and western faces were auspicious, whereas the southern face meant the destruction of progeny.'[6] We take in whatever vision of this auspicious side of the great linga is granted to us.

Fine, spray-like waterfalls from different sides flow into the stream, Lha Chu, on our left, giving it a greater body of water than it carries as it comes down from the north. It is as though the water has been sanctified by the Lord of Kailash and carried down by the mountains that look respectfully up to it. The mind feels withdrawn from any thought other than that of the strange environment which conveys an immense void. Mental prostrations to Shiva form the substratum of this thought.

There are many hallowed places around. There is a mountain which is known to be Hanuman, the loyal devotee of Rama. Soon we reach a place which is supposed to bear a footprint of the Buddha. As is the custom, we prostrate ourselves before it and perform a parikrama. It is believed that the kings of the three worlds appeared before the Buddha with treasures from their respective kingdoms. They asked him to give each one a statue of himself which they might keep and pray to, in their respective realms. Ravana, the king of the netherworld, took his statue back and worshipped it. But then he felt he needed a fitting pedestal for it. So he came to Kailash to lift the mountain on his back and carry it away to make a pedestal. Alarmed, five hundred deities came flying to the Buddha asking for his protection. Thereupon the Buddha stepped on the mountain in four places and fixed it there, stopping Ravana from carrying it. The four footprints are hallowed places on the four sides of the mountain.[7] This is the first one we encounter.

Myth and fact are blended in innumerable stories. Kerry Moran and John Russell circled the mountain and the lake several times in different seasons. Moran writes:

> This is a land where the supernatural naturally resides, and the veil separating ordinary reality from other realms draws even

> thinner at Kailash. As the trail moves northwards up the Valley of the Gods, the miraculous and the natural continually meet and merge, until the distinction between legend and fact, belief and truth, wavers and finally melts away altogether.[8]

After almost four hours we reach the next opening. We have crossed a narrow wooden bridge and gone to the western side of the stream. Most Tibetans continue to walk on its eastern side closer to the mountain, hugging its base. They will finish their *parikrama* sooner than us.

Our lunch as usual, is dry; I am glad I have my thermos of hot water. I make soup to replenish body fluids. The Tibetan yakwallahs – all men this time – are at home with their yak-dung fire and tea. They are going to stop for a long time.

Many Tibetans pass our way with small children trailing behind. A man with a starched white square-shaped headgear has an eight-month-old baby strapped to his back. His young wife who is a typist in Lhasa, walks alongside. The man is a doctor; we had met him in Dharchen. At the guesthouse we saw him sitting with a large box of multicoloured candy-like pills. Later we learned that the Chinese authorities appoint a Tibetan traditional doctor during this season for the welfare of the visitors. While the religious texts and scriptures were destroyed during the Cultural Revolution, the medical texts were left alone. The doctor is taking his mother and the rest of his family for the *parikrama*.

After the lunch break we have another four-hour walk ahead. But Li assures us that the monastery is just a little further. I feel happy to discover that we do better than the yaks, who are extremely slow. Those who ride, fall behind. When we are overtaken by a slight hailstorm, I wish to spot the riders behind us but there is no sign of them. 'They will come,' says Li. 'They are fast, you will notice their speed when we go up the slopes tomorrow. Then you will not be able to keep pace with them.' This first lap of the journey is about fifteen kilometres but it takes some of us almost eight hours. From 4,600 metres (15,200 feet) at Dharchen we climb up to more than 4,900 metres (16,200 feet) to reach Diraphuk monastery at 3 p.m. IST.

It is still bright daylight but the hail has brought a chill into the air. The younger ones, as usual, have reached before me. Hot tea is ready and waiting. Like at the other monasteries, we are given a straight row of four rooms. They are made of mud with a thick flat roof. There are thick mattresses on the floor with heavy quilts encased in clean white covers. Inside the room it is warm. The small square window with a broken pane does not deflect the warmth to any great extent.

About 500 feet above is the monastery of Zirebu or Diraphuk. The three syllables, Dorje had explained, symbolize specific things. *Zi,* or Chi, means that it is administered by the Chu Chi County. *Re*, is the symbol of the monastery and *Bo*, Bu or Phu, stands for cave. The name of the monastery can have another meaning also as Zi or Chi may mean holy yak, Re stands for holy horn and Bo or phu for cave. So it could be the cave of the holy horn or the holy yak. Built about 800 years ago, the monastery has a cave inside with a sign of the lion-faced yak that disappeared therein after showing the way to Chava Kotsang, the monk who is believed to have discovered the route around Kailash. This well-known Tibetan monk stopped at the base of Kailash, after finishing his *parikrama* of the Manas. As he tried to light a fire and make tea at the entrance of the canyon that leads up to Kailash, he felt he could not use any stone to prop up his kettle as each stone was inscribed with a Mani mantra. Just then he was guided through the mountain valley by a female yak who disappeared into this cave after revealing her real form, that of a *dakini*, or female spirit. Chava Kotsang is said to have prayed here for three years, three months and three days in the second decade of the thirteenth century, and a very small statue of his is enshrined here.

Like most others, this monastery has a special room reserved for monks who undertake *Shasana* (this Sanskrit word means discipline) during which they remain in the room for long periods, from one to three years. They do not step out to meet anyone. Food is supplied to them through a hole in the wall. Women are not allowed into the room. We are allowed to peek in from outside. Normally, even that is against the rule. Li asked the Tibetan doctor to accompany us here, as the lama in charge does not speak Chinese and Li knows no Tibetan. So the doctor translates for Li and Li translates for us. I wonder how much we lose out. But the lama is friendly and shows us all there is to see. There is one room where all the articles are stored. In the ante-room is the usual small window. It is directed straight into the opening between mountains – the north-west face of Kailash is a mass of snow hanging far above the surrounding mountains. Up a short flight of steps is an open balcony with its expansive wide-angle view of the mountains with Kailash at the centre.

The lama in the monastery is ill, and so, happy to meet the doctor. The temperature outside is several degrees below freezing point. We run back to our rooms for some warmth. Loh Sam, the lama who looks after our guesthouse, has a fire lit in his room. He has several kettles, some of which he generously loans out to us. He tells us stories about the caves and the building of the monasteries.

We cook and eat in the lama's room. He is generous with the hot water and in no particular hurry to put out the fire. Li tells me that the lama had run away from home when he was still a boy. He tried his hand at many things, even went to Hong Kong and worked as a mechanic. Then he changed his mind; he could not bear to see cruelty to living beings, and so became a monk. He has been here for many years; and performed seventy *parikramas* of the holy mountain. Of these, thirty *parikramas* were done for others – on payment. Most Buddhists, he says, would like to visit Bodh Gaya during the iron horse year. But he is sad because he cannot hope for a visit during this lifetime.

I bring him a small statute of Buddha filled with prayer things consecrated by the Dalai Lama at Bodh Gaya. I had received three statues with some consecrated holy pills from Rinpoche Doboom Tulku in Delhi. The lama is overwhelmed with joy. He reaches up on a shelf for a thick-framed picture, which he opens to draw out a number of articles. Who would have dreamt of so many sacred items hidden inside the frame! He gives me a beautiful metal badge with an image of Kailash and some old coins. 'You are a goddess from India. There have been many pilgrims from India, but none showed any interest in Tibetan customs and religion. He is very sorry that he has nothing to give to you to make up for the treasure you have given,' Li translates. Loh Sam goes on to tell Li that the treasure means more than 10,000 yuans to him. If someone asked him to choose between the money and this, he would choose this. The depth of his devotion is touching.

We talk about the next day's journey. We are to manipulate the Dolma Pass at a height of 5,600 metres (18,600 feet). I am concerned about my breathing. Li speaks to the Tibetan doctor and he has a medicine for my problem. The doctor gives me three pills, one to be taken before starting the journey, the second after crossing the first mountain, and the third after crossing the second mountain. He thinks I will make it without difficulty.

Loh Sam is happy to find receptive company. He fetches a long book, unbound like many Tibetan books, and says he will tell us how the weather will be tomorrow at Dolma when we cross it. The calendar he refers to is actually prepared for conditions in Lhasa, but he will try to work it out for this region. 'You will face a slight snow blizzard and cold winds, but you and your group will make it through.' I think of what I had read long ago, about a lama who could hold back the clouds and the snow for some time, to allow special visitors a passage through a difficult pass. Loh Sam is telling me we will do fine across the pass; he must know. It is almost two in the morning when I go to sleep. The thoughtful lama filled up my hot water bottle. We will start early on the long and tough journey tomorrow.

It is still dark. I hear someone enter the room, calling us in a gentle but deep voice, and placing a candle on the window sill. It is Loh Sam. Sleep at this time feels precious, but it must not continue. I come out of the room and sense something peculiar. Usually there is a bustle while tea is prepared, but this morning there is no such activity. In one of the rooms I find all the men snuggled in their beds, quiet. Strange. Silently, Desai goes into our room to ask for Durga's binoculars. What does he want to look at now when it is time to start? Finally, I discover that Surendra had gone out in the early hours of the morning and has still not returned. Satyam had gone with him, but he had started back when he found the mist too thick for visibility. Yesterday, Surendra had wanted to go to the base of Kailash, but he had been prevented from doing so because the mists were closing in and a hailstorm was upon us. Freezing from the cold, Satyam was now scared for the safety of his companion.

In the dense clouds that cover Kailash, it would be impossible to find him. We stretch our eyes into the mist and call out for Surendra in unison; our voice resounds through the mountains. The Tibetan pilgrims are already moving. 'My group will go through in safety,' I remind myself. I know Surendra will come, but until he does, no one is in a mood for any preparation. After a while, a yellow dot emerges in the distance. It is Surendra's jacket. The gait is unmistakable. We get ready for departure.

Surendra comes back with snow and small rocks from the base of the sacred mountain. He gives me some snow which I put in a bottle to take back for Lama Doboom Tulku. When I had asked him what would he like from the holy mountain, the Lama had laughed and said, 'Bring me some snow.' Perhaps he did not believe his desire would actually be fulfilled. I intend to refreeze it before presenting it to him in Delhi.

Our clothing today is heavy because of the sharp chill in the air. Li approaches me, 'Ma'am, have you taken your medicine?' My Chinese companion does not forget my requirements. I swallow one pill, as directed. Our path today is a series of steep climbs up to Dolma, the Pass we must cross before descending into the eastern side of Kailash. We go down for about half a kilometre and cross Lha Chu, the stream we have followed since our entry into the valley of the Amitabh Buddha. We now face the first climb; the yak men wait, hoping I will ride. I refuse. They continue to linger and cajole me every hundred yards or so. I refuse again, and again. Li walks with me. I will make it.

A little way up, I start getting short of breath. Li brings out something that looks like dried orange peel. 'Ma'am put this in your mouth and keep sucking on it.' The salty, tangy flavour of the Chinese medicine opens up the lungs and facilitates breathing. We walk slowly, observing people and the scenery, making short breaks so I can breathe easier. The yak men still hope I will ride. They are probably aware that the weather will not hold out for long; they want Li also to ride. We refuse. They are not happy. We are sure to be approached by them yet again.

As we climb, the rock and rubble which is Kailash, presents varied geological phenomena. Huge granite boulders line both sides of the path. The colour of rocks has changed to a deep-grey. The bright-red ended with the canyon of the Amitabha Buddha; we are now going through the valley of death. The colour is no longer warm and welcoming; the boulders on the path are massive. After one and a half kilometres we ford another stream, the Polung Chhu. Rare Tibetan herbs and incense material are obtainable here. The antiquity of the rocks and the rarity of the atmosphere have an impact on the flora which gives it medicinal properties. Tibetan medicine is known to use such herbs for a number of otherwise incurable diseases. Devotion as well as knowledge goes into the preparation of these medicines. *Soma*, the life-prolonging herb too, is believed to have been found here. The special herbs are said to be under the domain of Kubera who resides in these mountains by the side of Shiva. In the *Devi Mahatmayama* when various *devatas* offer their essential qualities which take the form of Devi to fight the demon Mahishasura, Kubera offers a vessel filled with *madhu*.[9] This *madhu* was none other than the juice of *Soma*[10], which gave her untiring strength to face the demon and his massive army.

A continuous line of Tibetans and their children moves on. A number of women walk with infants strapped to their backs. None makes a sound. It is as if the children too understand the sanctity of this pilgrimage. There are old women and men with wizened faces.

Another steep climb over scree and moraines brings us to an open area strewn with large boulders. It is the Shiva Tsaal, the place of rebirth. Here one faces Shiva, the Lord of time and death. To be born again one must first die. This is the symbolic culmination of the yatra. Tibetans lie down here and feign death. Offerings made here amplify the merit gained by performing the circumambulation. These are also said to ensure a place in the other world, or a rebirth in Tibet. Numerous prayer flags with the sacred mantra are scattered all over. Tibetans offer strands of hair, blood drawn from their gums, bits of food, just about anything. We observe a sock, a child's jacket, torn aprons and other things scattered haphazardly around. The small, worn-out garments present a bizzare sight against the majestic surroundings.

The Force that Unifies

> To see the greatness of a mountain, one must keep one's distance, to understand its form, one must move around it; to experience its moods, one must see it at sunrise and sunset, at noon and at midnight, in sun and in rain, in snow and in storm, in summer and in winter and in all the other seasons. He who can see the mountain like this comes near to the life of the mountain, a life that is as intense and varied as that of a human being.
>
> Lama Anagarika Govinda
> *The Way of the White Cloud*

Another steep ascent and we come to a big boulder. According to myth, it bears a footprint of the lion-faced yak that guided Chava Kotsang around the mountain. Tibetans make obeisance and recite their mantras around it with deep reverence and resonance. Instinctively, Li does the same. Charged with devotion, the atmosphere evokes an unpremeditated response in everyone. Li does not believe in

God, yet he too is unknowingly moved by the deep, simple faith that pervades the air.

At the top of the climb, we come upon a man facing Kailash and chanting mantras in Tibetan. A remarkable view of the mountain can be had from here, but it is cloudy and misty today. We only get a glimpse through a chink in the clouds. The sheer wall of snow, flanked by lesser mountains, towers almost 2,000 metres above the others. This rare view calls for offering special prayers. By the time I get close to the chanting Tibetan with my recorder he begins to move. We persuade him to chant some more. He goes back to the same spot and sings in his melodious voice. The song goes on and on. After several minutes we indicate to him that it is enough. He signals us to go on. He will finish it before resuming the walk.

We have seen innumerable stones and rock cairns carved with the sacred mantra, *Om mani padme hum.* Though commonly translated to mean 'Glory to the jewel in the lotus', it has a deeper connotation. Charles Allen writes:

> The first syllable represents the sound of enlightenment, the most fundamental of all mantras, and the last represents the sound of fulfilment. Encapsulated between the two is the phrase '*mani padme*', which does indeed translate as 'jewel in the lotus' but signifies '*lingam* in *yoni*' the mystical and sexual fusion of complementary opposites. It is the *yab* and *yum* united; Shiva and Shakti activated.[1]

The mantra is laid bare to the winds and sky, to be spread far and wide. The granite rock is hard. It must have taken a lot of time and effort to carve these inscriptions on rocks of all sizes. Writing came into Tibet with the sacred religion, so the written word too, is looked upon as sacred.

According to the Mahayana tradition, mantras are for the welfare of all. They invoke the powers-that-be to bestow all beings with health and happiness. Everything is shared and spread beyond the frontiers of the individual's limited being.

So is goodwill. Lama Anagarika reproduces what he read in a Tibetan lama's prayer book: 'I will act for the good and welfare of all living beings, whose numbers are as infinite as the expanse of the sky, so that, by following the path of love and compassion, I may attain to perfect enlightenment.'[2]

The benefit of the circumambulation is believed to be proportionate to the number performed. The same applies to the mantras which may be recited either verbally or spread into the firmament through other expeditious means like the prayer wheel. According to Tom Grunfield, 'Prayer wheels were particularly important for the premium placed on repetition.' In his book *Tibet and Tibetans*, Tom Grunfield presents the words of Shen Tsung-Lieu and Liu Shen-Chi:

> There are table wheels turned by the fingers; portable wheels turned by hands, tiny wheels turned by the winds; larger wheels propelled by man power; and the largest wheels of all, driven by hydraulic power. Wheels within wheels, whirling round and round. Imagine all the Tibetans muttering scriptures, continually walking around their monasteries, their cities, and their country where hundreds of thousands of such wheels are perpetually in motion.[3]

Even if numbers are given importance, the deep faith and sincerity with which prayers and *pradakshinas* are performed cannot but have a lasting impact on the personalities of those undertaking them. In an environment like this it is cynical to say that Tibetans believed only in the merit of quantity over quality of religious practices. The degree of tolerance noticed among Tibetans may be the result of their continuously repeating the mantra wherever they are.

On the same subject Lama Anagarika has written:

> The 'turning of the Wheel of the Dharma'... is a metaphor known to every Buddhist, meaning 'the setting into motion of the forces of the Universal and Moral Law', and in turning the prayer-wheel he becomes conscious of the supreme law which

> the Buddha proclaimed when he set the Wheel of Dharma rolling 2,500 years ago. For the Buddhist it is not sufficient that this act has been performed once by the Enlightened One – every single human being that strives for Enlightenment must repeat this creative act by realizing it in his own mind.[4]

He goes on to stress that prayers can be delivered by nothing other than the human heart. The mantra, its sound and meaning, do not aim at placating any powers located outside the heart. There can be no question of gaining favours from the gods by cheating them. Repeating mantras is an 'expression of the Supreme faith in the infinite power of goodwill and love that may act through an infinite number of means: through the thoughts of the wise, or the simple-hearted devotion of simple minds . . .'[5]

Due to the heavy screen of clouds the mountain is not visible much of the time, but its strongly-felt presence energizes the environment and charges the mantras with power. Like a magnetic force it connects all that stands and moves around it. Majestically clad in *akasha*, the subtlest element that signifies all matter, the mountain becomes the finest representation of spirit and matter coming together. Kailash was not born from the turbulent churning of dark subterranean forces that continue their movement under it, for it existed before them. It was raised to a level of transcendence by the crunching together of massive plates and made to appear like a radiant controlling power above them.

Our tired bodies do not allow strong mental impressions to be registered. But, there is a strong experience of existence – one's own and that of the mountain. Just Existence, at peace in the awareness of itself. It keeps us moving slowly. Like the vertical third eye of Shiva, the mountain stands transmitting benevolent radiance all around. The mind, at this stage, does not engage in extraneous thoughts. This would be the place where the third mental transformation could take place, as thought is stilled, giving place to just Beingness.

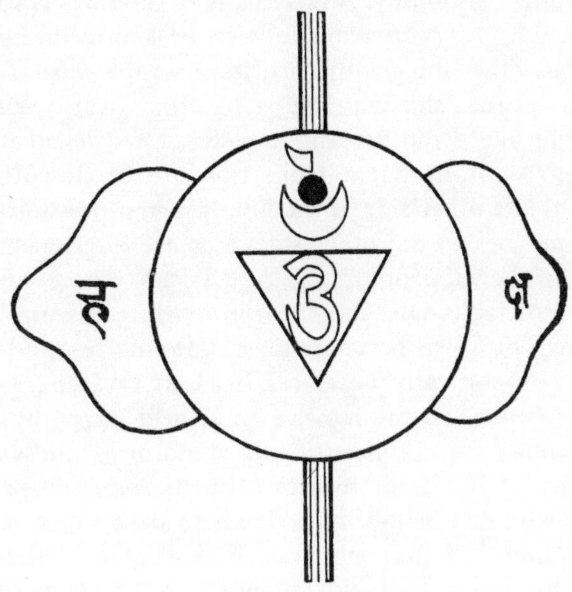

Ajna Chakra.

The women move on in their cheerfully coloured striped aprons made of Tibetan wool. I take photographs. Li waits patiently. I wonder at the warmth of this short-lived relationship without a common base – cultural, religious or ethnic. Instead, a layer that underlies surface differences of culture, language, nation or worldview has been touched. He has kept his word in remaining by my side, and is tolerant of the expressions of religious devotion.

Li and I believe we will join the rest of the group at the top of the pass, where they will halt to perform the ritual *puja*. The sky is darkening now and the pass must be crossed speedily. I spot a colourful canopy at the top where, I deludedly feel, we may get some refreshments. Getting closer, we find densely strung prayer flags that have taken on the appearance of a massive tent.

Dolma, the narrow pass and the Hill of Salvation, is marked by a large natural boulder. The large rock symbolizes Tara, the goddess of bounty. A miscellany of offerings is stuck on to the boulder — *tsampa*, bits of rice, broken teeth, beads and numerous other imaginative articles. Like the word Tara, Dolma also means 'she who helps to cross over'. She is compassionate like a mother and usually allows devotees to pass through without harm from this life to the other, symbolized by the other side of the hill. It is in a transformed body that one goes to the other side. Sins are forgiven here. This is unlike the Lipu or the Chang La Pass, whose ruling deity is unpredictable. One must not pray while crossing the Lipu as it may prove to be vengeful. But Dolma responds to prayers. Li automatically bows his head in reverence and touches his forehead to the massive rock, held sacred by the devout. Reverence for the majestic and grand in nature is not a religious act. It is a basic human instinct. Something in a place compels human beings to go down on their knees as an acknowledgement of that which is inexplicable, which is beyond the human capacity to comprehend. Scientists have not been spared such a feeling. Westerners, often not given to ritual belief or simple faith, have been struck by the stark, unearthly beauty of this area where contradictory elements coexist in harmony. Dorje told us the story of an Italian mountaineer who had wanted to climb Kailash. The Chinese authorities directed the European to him. Dorje asked the Italian to first circumambulate the mountain and then try climbing. After the *pradakshina*, the mountaineer came back and said, 'I cannot climb this mountain as every stone here is sacred.'

The Story of Punitvati

A twelfth-century text, Periya Puranam *tells the story of Punitvati, a very beautiful woman, who was a great devotee of Shiva. One day her husband left two mangoes in her safekeeping, as he wished to eat them later. In his absence, some Shaivite mendicants came to the house and Punitvati offered them the mangoes. When her husband returned, Punitvati produced a mango for him with her spiritual power. Her husband found the mango to be more delectable than anything he had had before. So he asked for the second one. Reluctantly Punitvati evoked her spiritual power again. This time the mango disappeared just as her husband was about to eat it. Realizing that Punitvati had supernatural powers, the terrified husband left her, married another woman and settled down in another village.*

Punitvati undertook severe austerities while praying to Shiva; she was revered as Karaikkal Ammaiyar on account of the skeletal form she acquired due to her penance. Her appearance resembled that of the ganas – the ghoulish attendants of Shiva. Karaikkal Ammaiyar then walked to Kailash, the abode of Shiva. As she felt the earth there was too sacred to be stepped on, she went around the mountain on her head. According to myth, Karaikkal Ammaiyar is present wherever the cosmic dance of Shiva is performed.[6]

Li is touched by the simplicity of the Tibetan people. Yet his Chinese conditioning forbids him from seeing them as beautiful. The values they uphold in their daily lives are different from his own – 'These people are so simple and pure, but so unlovely.' He cannot stand their food – 'They even eat raw meat. The girls, when they cook, keep biting off from the uncooked portions. Their lifestyle too, is different. I am used to bathing everyday.' I tell him that they cannot afford baths everyday as water is scarce and difficult to procure. 'No, some of them are very rich. They just don't want to,' he says. Perhaps the Chinese dislike of Tibetans is also based on their being a nationally and culturally distinct people, with their own beliefs and values.

Many Tibetans go around the mountain performing the *namaskar pradakshina*, prostrating themselves flat on their bellies for the entire path. They wear waterproof aprons in front to prevent getting wet when they prostrate their way across streams and waterways. Their hands are covered in waterproof mitten-like pieces open from the back, so as to look like hand-slippers. Carefully and with agility, they move about two steps after getting up so as not to go beyond the point where their fingertips had reached during the prostration. This point is marked by a little stone. Every inch of the sacred ground is covered by the prostrated body. They chant mantras throughout and are oblivious of passers-by. During the *pradakshina* period, they survive on *tsampa* and refrain from talking, as both the mind and speech are kept engaged with the mantra.

The intensity of the snow blizzard that started earlier increases as we reach the top of the pass. We had seen our co-travellers at the pass from a distance, but as we reach the top they are all gone. The puja must have been performed hurriedly. At this point, Li begins to have a bad backache. He has had no rest between guiding our two groups of yatris. The previous group was here only two days ago. The altitude, cold and exhaustion have taken their toll and depleted him of energy. He is dizzy. We keep moving slowly.

There is a drop beside the narrow path, below which we can see an emerald green lake. This is Gauri Kund, Parvati, daughter of Himavan is said to have come for her bath when the devatas prayed to her for protection, as described in the eleventh chapter of the *Devi Mahatmayam.*

Parvati – the purified one

Himavan represents the coming together of five elements to form gross matter. Matter also refers to the human body. Parvati, the daughter of the mountain, represents the energy that holds these elements together and imbues them with life. Desiring union with Shiva, the Lord of Kailash, the pure white mountain of snow, represented by the higher chakras

> *in the human body, Parvati had to undertake lengthy austerities. An incarnation of Sati who exhumed herself in yogic fire, Parvati is representative of shraddha or total devotion. Sati, the daughter of Daksha, a proficient but proud son of Brahma the creator, was married to Shiva. It was her stubbornness which took her to a yagya performed by her father. Seeing that no place had been reserved for her husband when all other gods and rishis had been provided their due places she burned herself with her yogic powers. This act of Sati symbolizes a suspension of ego and a surrender of the doubting mind as she had gone to her father's yagya against the counsel of Shiva, her husband. It was in the form of Parvati that she purified herself of egotistic doubts and joined back with the consciousness that forever descends to enliven matter.*[7]

At 6,000 metres (18,400 feet), the lake is said to be the highest fresh-water lake in the world and the most sacred. We do not consider going down 300 feet to bathe or collect water. The lake remains frozen almost all year round and the upper layer of ice must be broken if one dares take a dip.

After crossing the pass, we face a sheer drop. The path winds through boulders, streams and narrow passages through rock debris. The rest of our group is nowhere to be seen. But a little later, we can see Bhairavi going down laboriously with Surendra's help. He has both the patience and stamina to lead her through this difficult terrain, where riding on yaks is not possible. Tibetans have a saying – an animal that cannot take a rider up a slope is no animal and a man who cannot walk down a slope is no man. Yaks cannot carry human load here, the danger of falling is very real. All our people, except this tenacious old lady, have had several falls – some as many as eight.

We catch up with the two and try to give a hand, but it is not possible for two people to walk alongside on the narrow path. Standing lower down on the scree to help can also result in slipping uncontrollably. Somehow, Bhairavi is helped down to the path which opens out into a meadow. The others were to wait for us here but there is no one. I cannot even see the yaks, but Li spots them under an escarpment. We place the lady, ballooned in her raincoat, under a rock that bears a footprint of the Buddha. Tibetans hold it to be extremely sacred. The leader of our yak men comes up running, takes Bhairavi's hand and leads her to another rock. He also wants us to hurry; the weather is uncertain and more delay can cause problems. I pour out some hot water, steep it with glucose and pour it into Bhairavi's comatose mouth. Some almond biscuits and dates also come in handy. After the drink and the snack, she seems better. The yak men are quite willing to take her on animal back. The others have had to move on foot. We do not eat because there is no time.

Though the ground is quite flat now, one has to ford several streams and walk through marshy land in the valley of the Lamchu river. We understand now why yatris are allowed back onto their yaks only after a kilometre or more from this place. We are cajoled once again to ride; again, we decline. By now I am exhausted. The late night, the lack of sufficient nutrition and the difficult journey are telling on me. We make a short stop to have some dried fruits and hot soup.

My body wants to move no further, I want to stop here just as some Tibetans do. They carry their tents and are able to create a warm and comfortable space when everything around them is freezing and windy. Their brightly-coloured garments have surely been devised to counter the grey surroundings. If it is superstition and faith that provide strength and forbearance then it must be said that their faith is actually moving through mountains. The Chinese who wish to bring their brand of development to Tibetans say: 'Education out of superstitions – the bedrock of ignorance and conservatism – is not easy.'[8] Whether such education will make the Tibetans hardier, or give them greater courage to cope with the environment, is a question that goes abegging.

The Chinese look upon an assignment in Ngari as a punishment as there is neither water nor fuel, nor proper food. But Tibetans with their faith survive happily, sending out good wishes for the welfare of all humanity.

The cold gives a purple tinge to the furrowed faces of the Tibetans. The rarefied oxygen demands an increase in the red blood cells. As a result, even the Chinese who have lived here long, tend to look a bit like the Tibetans. Li tells me that some of the Tibetans smear their cheeks with a mixture of goat blood and yak butter to prevent their skins from cracking. The goat blood, when it cracks after coagulation looks dark and furrowed, he says.

Yatra – an ascent in the mind

We continue to turn around the bends in the mountain ranges. The end is nowhere in sight. Unlike the lake region, this area arouses no expectation of a goal or a destination. As a matter of fact, there is no sign of any goal. Having reached the top it looks as though there is nowhere to reach. The 'reaching', if any, is in one's own mind. While Kailash and its environs provide the optimum physical conditions for experiencing the transcendent, the experience itself has to arise within one's own consciousness. The yatra erodes predetermined notions and conditioning, allowing space for the experience to shine through, just as Kailash shines through the mass of dark forces that tumefy under it. That is the only role that the journey plays. It lets one know that the destination resides in the heart of the pilgrim. When that is realized the external symbols and the objective destination cease to exist. The journey culminates in shedding the sense of exteriority. The destination and the traveller do not any more remain two separate realities.

The sun is beginning to set, and my steps are heavy and laboured. The continuous descent has strained my back and limbs. Surendra tries to help, but not much can be done. The orange glow of the sun touches the mountains with gold. We are enveloped in a surreal translucence. If it were possible to drop sail wherever one wanted, then this would be the point for me.

We are worried about our people ahead, as they would surely be about us. Possibly we are three kilometres from the camp, but no one has sent even a yakman to check on us. Darkness falls suddenly. Li has a torch and the small beam helps. Besides, there are no frightening precipices here, no boulders or big rocks any more. The path just seems endless even while we question the whole idea of a destination. We peer out into the dark trying to spot a torch looking for us. None appears. The walk continues.

It is past eight o'clock. Another hour and we will be there. In the pitch dark at about nine o'clock, we spot a faint glimmer of light. The camp cannot be far. On reaching there all is gloomy and quiet, there is no sign of welcome. They waited so anxiously for us that they did not even cook dinner. Our arrival creates a mixed response – of relief and annoyance. Desai brings some Threptin biscuits. Durga gets up to make some soup. We ask her not to. Everyone gets into their beds and goes off to sleep. The keeper of this guesthouse has lived in Banaras and speaks good Hindi. He is a surly fellow, but somehow he agrees to fill my hot water bottle. The water is tepid, but I am grateful for even this much warmth. The room is dark and I cannot find my torch. The emollient for sore muscles cannot be located but balmy sleep takes over.

Zuthulphuk Gompa

We wake up in the morning to an unrecognizable white landscape. All the peaks are covered with a soft layer of snow and a spray of snowflakes continues. We are slow to start – the journey today is only about thirteen kilometres, and it is a gradual descent most of the way. Tea is prepared at a leisurely pace.

As we sip tea and soak in the freshness of the mountains we suddenly feel we have seen an apparition. Loh Sam, the lama, from the previous monastery appears before us. We greet him warmly. He hands me the torch that I left behind. I am grateful and ask Li to find out the reason for his coming here. 'He says he came to give you the torch, he felt that you would require it. You still have some way to go.' He started at 3.30 in the morning (it is now almost eight). I am touched. My mind conjures up images of the 'flying' lamas described by many a writer. Alexandra David Neel in her *Magic and Mysteries of Tibet* speaks of lamas who can cover vast distances in a short time as they have perfected the technique of *Lung-gom*, of filling their bodies with air and becoming light, so that when they walk they appear to be in a trance and their rhythmic steps do not seem to touch the ground they traverse. Guiseppe Tucci had also ruefully noticed that the Manasarovar *parikrama,* which took him ten days, could be accomplished in one day by 'adepts with the power to cover enormous distances by means of long, floating strides while in a state of trance . . .'[9] Lama Anagarika writes:

> The deeper meaning of *lung-gom* is that matter can be mastered by the mind . . . In the case of *lung-gom,* the adept is required to concentrate on all the phenomena, aspects and functions of the vital element air. *Gom (sgom)* means meditation, contemplation, concentration of mind and soul upon a certain object, as well as the gradual emptying of the mind of all subject-object relationship, until a complete identification of subject and object has taken place.[10]

Loh Sam has made the journey in about four hours, through the dark of night with snow falling continuously. Of course he has gone around the mountain many times so there is no reason to think that he cannot do it so fast. After all, don't the Tibetans do the whole *parikrama* in one day? Yet I think of my own laborious journey.

I regretfully tell him that I have no way of repaying him for the trouble he has taken and offer him some chocolates. But the lama only wants some medicine for a headache, and then starts back. I feel overwhelmed.

Another hour and a half passes by the time we make a move after a breakfast of biscuits and cheese. There are not many in the group who are keen to visit the Zuthulphuk Gompa – the monastery of the miracle cave. It means an extra climb of a hundred metres or so. Some of us go up, and we find for the first time, other pilgrims, Tibetans, praying inside. The lama does not want photographs to be taken. I give him some of the pills consecrated by the Dalai Lama and insist that he allow us to photograph him. He says he is too old and ugly. I tell him I want to take his picture to India. He takes time to preen himself and then stands in front of the small library of manuscripts that his monastery still has.

In the dark corridors on both sides of the central aisle, there are Tibetans prostrating or sitting and chanting mantras. In front is a statue of Milarepa in the famous posture – right hand cupped near his right ear listening to the cosmic sound, while the left hand on his knee holds a bowl of nettle soup, the only food on which he lived in these freezing surroundings. On one side is the small cave in which Milarepa meditated. Milarepa chose this cave as a suitable place for meditation, but he found it too small and cramped. So, according to myth, he pushed the ceiling up with his hands. Due to an error in judgement it got pushed too far up, and that made the cave too drafty and cold. So he went up and pressed the roof down with his foot. The foot print above and the hand print inside the cave are still there!

Milarepa

Milarepa, the mystic poet of the late eleventh and early twelfth century (A.D. 1040-1123), was called Repa because he chose to wear just one undyed cotton cloth. Due to the practice of *tummo* (inner heat), he was able to survive the extraordinary cold. During his sojourn in this region, where he undertook severe penance, he lived on nettles.

Milarepa was the disciple of the famous scholar-translator, Marpa (A.D. 1012-1096), who together with Brogmi (A.D. 992-1072), was a fountainhead of the *Sa-skya* and *bKa'-rgyud* orders. As they gave importance to the magical and miraculous aspects of Buddhist practice, the two teachers avoided meeting Atisha who laid emphasis on austerities and inner purity.[11] Marpa spent a total of sixteen years with his teacher Naropa, in his hermitage at Pulahari in Bihar. Naropa's teacher was the famous Tilopa from Kashmir. After learning various magical practices and the Buddhist doctrine, Marpa settled down to a life of a householder in southern Tibet. Milarepa was subjected to severe disciplines by his teacher. These included the labour of building and rebuilding a nine-storeyed stone tower. The perseverance and sincerity of Milarepa won him the compassion and kindness of Marpa's wife, Nairatmya. That is what sustained him during the period of harsh discipline imposed on him.[12]

A number of myths about Milarepa's life are connected to the Kailash-Manasarovar region. It is said that Milarepa first went to Kailash in A.D. 1093 where he competed many times with Naro Bonchung, a powerful Bon priest. Till then, according to Choying Dorje, our guide, the history of Tibet had been one of conflict between the followers of Bon, the pre-Buddhist shamanistic religion of Tibet, and Buddhism, the religion brought here from India. As a last test of power, the Bon priest challenged Milarepa to reach the summit of Mount Kailash before him. This was to be the final battle which would determine, once and for all, the end of Bon supremacy over the area. It would make the mountain a place associated with the Buddha and the various deities appropriated by Tibetan Buddhism from the Bon and Hindu religions. As the competition began the Bon priest huffed and puffed and started to climb. He climbed through the night without stopping even once. Much to the consternation of his followers, Milarepa sat unperturbed. Just as the first ray of the sun came out he became a part of the ray through intense concentration and reached the top of the mountain in a wink. According to another version of the myth, Milarepa turned his cotton shawl into wings and flew to the summit. On seeing Milarepa already there, just as he was about to make it to the top, the Bon magician got such a shock that his little *damaru* fell from his hand and went clanking down the mountain. The step-like striations on the south face of the mountain are believed to be the indentations caused by the *damaru.* The striations are also a sign of the takeover of Kailash by Buddhists from the followers of Bon.

Despite his achievements, Milarepa was considered an embarrassment to the few relatives he had because he wore practically no clothes, lived like a pauper, and was undeterred by worldly concerns. When his sister came to see him in such conditions, she urged him to wear something more decent and eat proper food. He answered in verse, telling her not to feel concerned. He apprised her of his attainments saying:

> High in this lonely rock gorge
> Nothing eases my constant melancholy,
> And such melancholy is inseparable
> From the enlightenment of holy lamas.
> As a result of my great effort
> There is no doubt my spiritual understanding grows.

Milarepa did not take many disciples; Gampopa is the best known. Because of Milarepa's association with the ka-rgyu, or Black Hat sect, followers of this order frequent the mountain more than others. He is said to have died in a cave on the shores of Lake Manasarovar.[13]

At the End of the Spiral

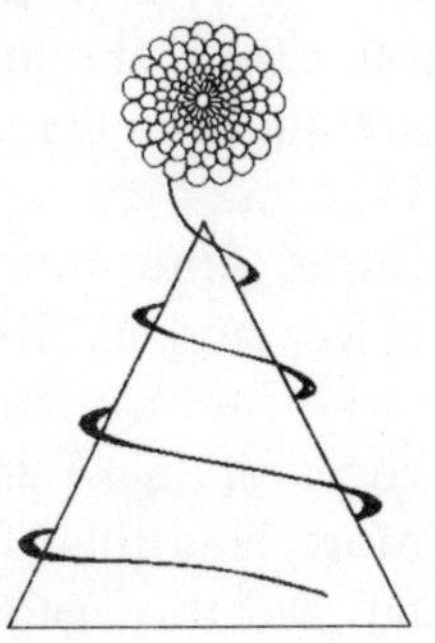

We shall not cease from exploration
And the end of all our exploring
Will be to arrive where we started
And know the place for the first time.

T.S. Eliot
Four Quartets

We walk at a leisurely pace. There is no rush any more. This is the last day we will be walking in this area, the journey back will be in a bus or truck except for the last trek up to Lipu when we finally leave Tibet. Many more Tibetan women with their children are visible today. They too look relaxed and happy. It has stopped snowing, and the sun is up. The mountain peaks make for an enchanting backdrop to the grassy valley we walk through. On the left is a stream going down to Dharchen. It will join the Sutlej via the Rakshasa Tala.

After two hours, we come upon a natural rock shelter which must provide comfort to many a soul caught in unexpected storms. Near the shelter is another place sacred to the Tibetans. On the rock, there is supposed to be an elbow imprint of a woman who lay down here and died of exhaustion while performing her thirteenth round of the mountain. When she had offended the deities by giving a drink of water from Gauri Kund to her nine-month-old infant, she had vowed to make thirteen rounds of the mountain. After the completion of the thirteenth round, her infant (who had died) was to be brought back to life. Had this been an Indian folk tale such a woman would probably have been rewarded with the life of her child, and she herself with divine status. But here in Tibet, she is allowed to die while completing the promised thirteenth round. The place is held to be holy by the Tibetans. We make our obeisance and take photographs of the happy children sitting in front of the rock face.

The yaks gambol up and down the mountain slopes. The yak men make sure Bhairavi is on a yak, even when the others are asked to dismount on dangerous terrains. From this side, we cannot get even a glimpse of Kailash. Yet it remains in the mind. Four hours later an encouraging sight emerges far below and in front of us. The Rakshasa Tala appears like a large saphire shimmering against the golden ground. The edges of the Tala look much more dramatic and its waters more blue than the Manasarovar. The destination cannot be far. But this again is an illusion; we will perhaps have to walk another few hours before we get there.

As we near the camp at Dharchen, we notice some more *mani* stones along the way. These are the offerings made by the diligent and devoted though unknown pilgrims after the successful completion of the circumambulation. The mountain has been looked upon as a *mandala* by the Buddhists, with each side presenting a different personality. Lama Govinda writes:

> He [the pilgrim] approaches the mountain from the golden plains of the south, from the noon of life . . . He enters the

> red valley of Amitabha in the mild light of the sinking sun, goes through the portals of death between the dark northern and the multi-coloured eastern valleys when ascending the formidable Dolma-La, the Pass of Tara, the Saviouress – and he descends, as a newborn being, into the green valley of Aksobya on the east of Kailash . . . the pilgrim again emerges into the open, sunny plains of the south, assigned to the Dhyani-Buddha Ratnasambhava, whose colour is that of gold.[1]

Finally, we sight the tents that make up the village or township of Dharchen. We walk into one of the tents at the edge of the village. A young Chinese boy, with clever narrow eyes welcomes Li. In front of the tent there are shelves lined with tinned fish, canned meat, matchboxes, drinks and torches. It is both his home and place of work. He wants to palm off a second-hand camera of dubious make to Li. He is very persuasive, but Li holds back. We have a can of Coca-Cola for eight yuan each. After our little break we move towards the familiar row of white-washed rooms that make up our camp.

It is evening and the sky is bright. Tomorrow we depart, so it's time to look for souvenirs to take back. Having completed the *parikramas* successfully, the mind feels light. Through the human manure that surrounds the camp, we walk to the tents that form the market. The shops offer cloth from India, and there are the ubiquitous red thermos flasks. They sell quite cheaply, each costing the equivalent of sixty rupees. There are narrow strips of woven, striped wool; Tibetan women join these to make aprons which they wear over their dresses. There are dark glasses in fancy leather cases.

Beads, mostly imitation, of turquoise and coral, are strung together as *malas*. We buy some. The women are hard bargainers. They would rather forego selling than reduce the price quoted, however unrealistic it may be. The attitude is similar to what we encountered in the upper regions of the Himalayas on the other side.

In the evening, Dorje comes and tells us that he has not seen a group as harmonious as ours. It feels good even though he may be saying it just to please us. He says it must be due to the sense of devotion with which the group is imbued. He wishes to give a certificate, but he is thinking about how he should word it in English. The six of us who have performed the *parikrama* on foot get beautiful certificates, each with a picture (from Varanasi) symbolizing the cycle of life. A little later, he brings a copy of the journal (written in Tibetan by him), about the Kailash-Manasarovar region and its importance. It is wrapped in a white muslin *khatta* and presented to me. Inside there is a note saying this is the first group in which not a single yatri was kept back from either of the *pradakshinas,* and in which a total of eleven people performed the Kailash *parikrama* on foot. As the coordinator of the yatra at this end and being a religious man, he feels this is an achievement to be reckoned with and that it could not have been done without the blessing of the gods.

Back to Purang

In the morning Garry arrives to take us back to Tseti, where we get together with the other half of the group. Dorje is taking his relatives back, so he will follow us in a truck. There is excitement at having completed the yatra, and jadedness at having to traverse the same road a fourth time. We prevail upon Garry to take the bus down to the stream where we can take one last direct look at the mountain from the south-west. The day is relatively clear, and the mountain reveals itself in its full glory. The group piles out into the blistering cold morning to take photographs. I mentally recite a last prayer. The heart is sad, though fulfilled. Will there ever be another encounter with this living presence? Two people in the group are visiting here for the second and third times. But I am not sure about being able to repeat the yatra. The satisfaction at having been allowed this opportunity and the body having withstood it, brings a sense of gratitude. There is a feeling of protection all around. People have been loving and helpful, going out of their way to make our yatra successful.

The sun is still young in the day, as we resume our ride. A searing cold wind blows right through our skins. I do not have my balaclava out; I don't like wearing it anyway. So Li detaches the furlined hood of his jacket and places it over my head. It is extraordinarily warm. I had not realized that the furs Tibetans wear are so protective. No wonder they are able to brace the cold.

At Tseti, some wish to take another dip in the holy lake. Desai and others in the group coax Li to join them. He hasn't ever taken a dip.

Tripathiji finds a beautifully crafted copper ring in the waters and slips it onto my little finger. My reservations about accepting someone else's property are set aside. Anything washed by the holy waters is worthy of veneration and should be received with humility, he says. A large number of water bottles and jerry cans we had ordered are ready and waiting, filled with the holy water.

The atmosphere at Purang is relaxed, but Rudram looks exhausted and weak. He complains of a headache and dizziness and refuses to eat. His co-yatris looked after him as best as they could, but he still does not feel well. Two of the older yatris are worried about their own well-being; Rudra is feverish so they wouldn't like to share a room with him. Sundaram moves out of his room, offering his bed to the sick man. Ghanashyam does not mind sleeping next to Rudram. In fact he looks after him, boosts his morale with his healing techniques, and gives him a sedative. In the morning, we are headed towards Khojarnath, the monastery on the border with Nepal.

Khojarnath

Once again, we scramble onto a truck. This time however, it is possible to use a chair as a stepping stool. The way to Khojarnath rolls south-eastward. We watch small-sized farms, maturing crops and small tractors here and there. Water has been channelized from nearby streams for the purpose of irrigation. The soil appears to be fertile. A village here means a cluster of four or five mud structures. We see horses and yaks, too.

It takes about three hours to reach Khojarnath, twenty kilometres away from the Purang guesthouse. At Khojarnath, we go through a narrow alley between mud walls; on one side there is an open drain with clean, flowing water. At the end of the alley we enter the monastery through a huge gate. The shrine is located in a large building in the centre of a rectangular courtyard. The building is locked. Someone goes to call the lama in charge and, in the meantime, we explore the outside. The front door is guarded by fierce-looking deities. On the left is Tamdin, the fierce form of Avalokitesvara who represents compassion and purity. And on the right is Chagdor, the fierce form of Amitabha or the Dhyani Buddha. The side walls are lined with massive, three-foot-high brass prayer wheels enclosed behind iron bars. Walking past, the prayer wheels can be turned serially, by putting one's hand through the bars, setting all of them into motion. The yard is sunny and the brass wheels are touched golden by the light.

On the rear side of the monastery is the seat, or *gaddi*, of Lotsava (translator) Rinchen Tsangpo whom Atisha met when he visited the Guge kingdom. He delivered lectures from here for twelve years. Atisha, too, spent a season here before proceeding to Tholing at Guge, via Manasarovar. A little further away flows the Karnali river. A bridge across the Karnali leads into Nepal.

Finally, the door of the shrine is opened. We enter a large dark hall, at the end of which are three statues, breathtaking in their beauty. Claimed to be made of silver, they stand on pedestals of lotus flowers carved from the *ashtadhatus*, or eight metals. The delicate smiling faces with sensitive expressions have led Indian pilgrims to believe they are statues of Rama, Lakshmana and Sita. But, Swami Pranavananda clarifies that they are all male deities. The one in the middle – eight feet high, with a yellow face – is Manjughosha, a symbol of spiritual knowledge. On his right is Avalokitesvara, seven feet high; and on his left is Chagan Dorje, or Vajrapani, the one who holds a thunderbolt in his hand and is usually seen as a protector. This also is seven feet high. According to Swami Pranavananda, the statues were sculpted in the southern Indian style by Nepali sculptors.[2] It is also said that in 1899, a fire severely damaged the two statues on either side of Manjugosha. These were then rebulit by Nepali, Kashmiri and Tibetan sculptors. A wonderful story of cultural integration!

The walls of the inner sanctum depict old paintings. The ceiling too is covered with the rich glow of paintings. It is a wonder that quite a few paintings are still intact. During the cultural revolution, this hall had been turned into a godown and the rest of the monastery into party offices. Many of the artefacts are supposed to have been hidden away, and so saved from destruction. Outside, we notice some broken statues. Several thoughts run through my mind. Belief, which has sustained them through centuries of harsh life, has also enabled the Tibetans to wade through the cultural invasion without losing faith. Could development be brought about by destroying the work of a thousand years? Why can't humans respect different beliefs and work through them to carry out their ideas of progress? Would such a process not be enriching for all?

A number of Nepalis come in; an old lama recites a prayer for them. They stand with hands folded, concentrating fully on the sound. One of the children looks in my direction as I move closer to listen, and a watchful father quietly turns his head teaching him to listen intently to the invocation.

In another part of the monastery, there is only one massive idol of Mahakala in a large bare hall. According to Swami Pranavananda there were numerous other images here – a beautiful one of Maitreya, the future Buddha, and one of the Devi in the form of Tara. There was also a large prayer wheel – ten-foot high and eight feet in diameter. The paintings on the walls here have been completely destroyed. Renovation work is now in progress, and some new ones are being painted over the destruction. The loud garish colours of the new works contrast sharply with the rich mellowness of the original ones in the shrine. The whole culture, if it ever comes alive again, would be different. Tibetan tolerance and faith in their ability to survive keep them from blaming anyone. They strive to slowly build again.

We are given lunch at the guesthouse when we get back late in the afternoon. I would have liked to go to the Nepali *mandi*, a little beyond the monastery, but I do not have the strength to walk another five kilometres. The younger ones go out shopping. After a while, Li comes back swinging a bluish folding umbrella in his hand. He hands it to me, saying he could not get anything 'real' here. He would send me some thing 'real' from Nanjing. He bought this because he remembered my broken umbrella in Dharchen.

Rudra continues to feel sick, and he does not respond to the medicines we administer. Garry says we can take him to the local hospital. There is still the Lipu Pass to be negotiated before we can begin to feel we are homeward bound. We decide to go to the hospital in the morning. Garry organizes a Toyota station wagon. I ask Surendra to accompany us.

I did not expect much to happen in the whitewashed mud building located in the middle of a dusty path. The hospital is clean though somewhat empty looking. The receptionist asks for five yuans as registration fee. She makes a card and we are led to the doctor. A simple *bokhari* spreads its warmth in the room. The doctor examines Rudram and prescribes medicine. 'Is he Chinese?' I ask. 'No, didn't you realize we were speaking Tibetan?' Garry's voice carries the sound of hurt pride. 'I told you that we are now slowly beginning to manage things ourselves. All the staff here is Tibetan.'

We pay another ten yuans for the medicine – for the locals it is free – and then go into a room where two women stand, wearing gauze masks. They ask Rudram to sit, and one of them begins to fill a syringe, the size one associates with injecting large animals. Then she fills another syringe. I feel alarmed and ask what it is. Garry is in another room, perhaps fulfilling some more formalities. She reassuringly shows me the vials; I cannot read the print but it seems to be B_{12}. Through gestures, they ask me to trust them. One of the women approaches Rudram with an injection. Surendra and I try to distract him. She asks him repeatedly if he has eaten something. We say he hasn't, but she feels it would be all right. One syringe is slowly emptied into Rudra's arm, and then the second one is attached to the same needle. He complains of dizziness. They go on till he can bear it no more. Before they stop he slips down from the chair – eyes rolled up and the body stony and stiff. Immediately, the needle is pulled out. A rubber pillow with a narrow tube serves as an oxygen cylinder. The tube is pushed up Rudra's nostril, while his mouth is held closed. Garry is in by now. I am struck by momentary panic. 'Don't worry,' they find time to soothe me. With alacrity they lift Rudra and stretch him out on a bench. His body is cold and wooden. My heart raises a prayer, 'Oh Shiva, what are you doing now, at this last moment when the whole journey has ended?' A voice inside replies, 'Who are you to panic? You are not the doer. You are not responsible for all that has happened. If you have been made in charge, it does not mean you run the show.'

Surendra and I rub Rudra's hands and feet till they become warm. That gives hope. The doctor also comes in. Garry holds the oxygen pipe deftly as though he is used to it. Soon one pillow is emptied. Another one, perhaps their last, is used. 'Have we been too late?' asks my mind. Cerebral oedema can lead to the end within hours, I have read.

One of the women pushes another needle in his buttock. I feel apprehensive while two more injections go into his body. The nurses seem reassured. At this point it occurs to me to check out on fact and reality from drama and fright. When I ask him to move his hand, Rudra lifts his arm slowly. It is difficult not to laugh. The relief and the comic nature of the situation suddenly strikes us all.

Like a true Indian, Surendra thinks of giving him some tea. The hospital cannot provide it, but very quickly someone fetches a flask of hot buttered tea. A bowlful is poured out. Rudra drinks it thirstily. Another bowl and another. When the fourth is being poured out, an embarrassed Surendra says we will get some more at the guesthouse. But Rudra wants it. Filled up with the rejuvenating fluid, he looks happy and energized. Relieved, we finally leave the hospital. The air outside is fresh. We breathe freely once again.

Back at the guesthouse, the waiting shoppers are disappointed. They have no idea of the panic and consternation we have lived through. No shopping is possible now because the return journey starts early next morning. All Chinese currency is collected and reconverted to Indian rupees. All bags, except a small overnighter retained by each, are checked in. The officials do not care to open and examine any bag, but the formalities must be completed. The journey at this end is practically over. In the morning, we will cross Lipu and step back into Indian territory.

Lipu Again

It is approximately 2.30 a.m. The sky is a dark star-studded dome. Everything is quiet. Garry has organized a couple of extra cars to bring back the forty yatris who form the next group. A little later Li comes and slips a lump of Chinese medicine into my coat pocket, 'for the journey across Lipu'.

There is plenty of wheeled transport to choose from, so I get into a Toyota Range Rover. The journey through a tranquil pall of darkness induces a stupor. The expert Chinese driver is on the bus. We get a novice. Half an hour later, we ford a strong current of water flowing over high boulders. The baggage truck, the bus and the other car have gone past, but we are stuck – there is a great revving sound but no movement. The water flows with raging fury all around us. After several minutes of unsuccessful struggle, the expert driver of the bus arrives. He gets into the car and dexterously frees it from the hold of the boulders. The hurdle cleared, we continue our journey under the living, protective presence of Shiva.

As the Flow Continues

> Man, in his physical body, is but a halting place, a condensation that *prakriti* deposits on earth, before this body is dissolved and annihilated.
>
> Stella Kramrisch
> *The Presence of Shiva*

Metaphorically we have completed a journey from the world of desire, with its multifarious attractions, to the world (paradoxical as it may sound) of moksha, where only the unity of existence is manifested. We have passed through the sphere of time into that of the Timeless. In the vast supernal flux of nature and infinity, products of the human mind are but specks that flicker and fade away into the Great Potential from which they may appear again. We have passed through Himalayan ranges, alive with the fiery energy of the elements. We have seen that spirit and matter are not two disparate entities but that they mingle and enliven each other in every sphere. That the transcendent continuously vibrates through the immanent.

We have gone around the ultimate symbol of Shiva radiating its centripetal force, and we have striven to stretch our minds in an attempt to experience Him as He is. For Shiva is not an entity outside of our being. He remains the 'witness established in the hearts of all beings'.[1]

We have seen that the social conditioning that shapes us is vulnerable to question; and that such conditioning often divides and separates us from other things and beings. But as this conditioning gets eroded in the presence of the great elements, our minds can expand to experience the unity that underlies the divisions. It is possible to understand, even experience, that the '*pasu*, the sentient being, freed from its fetters (*pasa*) no longer knows itself as separate from Shiva, while the *pasu*, ensnared by the world and its riches, may not be aware that Shiva is in him.'[2]

To get to the truth of this, we need to go beyond the conglomerate of rocks and stones that is Kailash to the potential it represents. We need to ruminate on the yatra long after the journey is over. The journey of the *spirit* begins after the physical ardour is over.

> God is here within us . . . and not there on the mountain: the mountain is no more than a heap of stones. But people cannot raise themselves instantly to the heights of our contemplation: the life of the spirit is an ascent – some begin from a long way off, some from nearby; but though the paths are various – and must of necessity be various, since men think, understand and feel in varying ways – though the paths are various, the point of arrival is one alone.[3]

'The point of arrival' cannot be reached through the intellect, by rational calculation, or even after a long and difficult physical journey.

> Each *pasu*, or living creature, is an exemplar of the life-principle. In their differentiated aspects, the *pasus* are numberless, and Shiva as the archetypal divine principle of life is the Lord of

> them all. The bonds that keep them together are known as *pasa.* Unless these bonds are loosened both by the grace of the Lord and the endeavour of the devotee, no one can get rid of them and the soul that is soiled by matter remains bound in the snares of death.[4]

By unfolding before us, and confronting us with the trivial as well as the eternal, the yatra provides us with an opportunity to choose the eternal. It is for us to make the choice.

References

Chapter 1

1. John Snelling, *The Sacred Mountain*, East West Publications, London, 1983, pp. 26-39.
2. Ibid., pp. 217-18.
3. *Vishnu Purana*, Gita Press, Gorakhpur, II.2.
4. As explained by A.P. Tiwary, Deputy Director General (Rtd), Geological Survey of India.
5. *Vidyesvarasamhita* XVI, pp. 87-90 in J.L. Shastri, ed., *Shiva Purana*, vol. I, Motilal Banarsidass, Delhi, 1970.
6. Ibid., XVIII, 19-23.
7. Ibid., XVII, 98-101.
8. Ibid., XVIII, 10-11.
9. Stella Kramrisch, *The Presence of Shiva*, Oxford University Press, New Delhi, 1981, p. 439.
10. *Srimad Bhagvatam*, Gita Press, Gorakhpur, Bk. VIII, ch. vii, Shloka 13-44.
11. Kapila Vatsyayana, ed., *In the Image of Man*, New Delhi, 1982, p. 213.
12. *Rudra Samhita* in *Shiva Purana*, 23. 16-17.
13. M.S. Poornalingam, *Ravana the Great*, Solden and Co. Printer, Madras, (publication date not known).
14. Stella Kramrisch, *The Presence of Shiva*, Oxford University Press, New Delhi, 1981, p. 154.
15. Lama Anagarika Govinda, *The Way of the White Cloud*, B. I. Publicaitons, Bombay, 1960, p. 61.

16. Parshotam Mehra, *The Youngsblood Expedition: An Interpretation*, Asia Publishing House, New Delhi, 1968, p. 19
17. As explained by A. P. Tiwary.
18. Charles Alfred Bell, *The People of Tibet*, London, 1928, p.1.

Chapter 2
1. Lama Anagarika, *The Way of the White Cloud*, B. I. Publications, Bombay, 1960, pp. 70-71.
2. Quoted in John Snelling, *The Sacred Mountain*, East West Publications, London, 1983, p. 108.
3. Quoted in Snelling, p. 131.
4. Swami Shivananda, *Lord Shiva and His Worship*, Divine Life Society, 1962, pp. 212, 215-16.
5. Swami Pranvananda, *Kailash Manasarovar*, Surya Print Process: New Delhi, p. 28.
6. Lama Anagarika Govinda, *The Way of the White Cloud*, pp. 63-64.
7. *Vidyeshwara Samhita*, in *Siva Purana*, XVIII, 149.

Chapter 4
1. Swami Krishnananda, *Spiritual Import of Religious Festivals*, The Divine Life Society, Rishikesh, 1982, pp.184-201.
2. Choying Dorje, *Buddhism in Tibet*, Translated from Tibetan for this book by Gyurme.

Chapter 5
1. *Vidyeshvara Samhita*, 132-34, in *Shiva Purana*.
2. Jai Deva Singh, *Shiva Sutras*, p. 83.

Chapter 7
1. John Snelling, *The Sacred Mountain*, East West Publications, London, 1983, pp. 209, 211.
2. Swami Krishnananda, *Spiritual Import of Religious Festivals*, The Divine Life Society, Rishikesh, 1982, pp.1868-7.

Chapter 8
1. V.S. Agrawal, *Shiva Mahadeva, The Great God: An Exposition of the Symbolism of Shiva*, Veda Academy, Varanasi, 1966, p. 36.

Chapter 9
1. *Yuddha Kandam*, 74. 29-74, in *Valmiki Ramayana*, Gita Press, Gorakhpur.
2. Explained by A.P. Tiwari, Deputy Director General (Rtd.), Geological Survey of India.

Chapter 12

1. Lama Anagarika Govinda, *The Way of the White Cloud*, p. 60.

Chapter 13

1. Swami Pranavananda, *Kailash Manasarovar*, 2nd Edition, New Delhi, 1983, p. 62.
2. *Ibid.*, p. 63.
3. *Ibid.*
4. A. Tom. Grunfeld, *The Making of Modern Tibet*, Oxford University Press, 1987, p. 29.
5. Swami Pranavananda, p. 76.
6. Jack Finnegan, *Tibet: A Dreamt of Image*, Tibet House, New Delhi, 1986, p. 9.
7. Giuseppe Tucci, quoted in Grunfeld, p. 24.
8. A. Tom. Grunfeld, p. 24.
9. *Ibid.*, p. 26.
10. Swami Pranavananda, p. 100.
11. Jack Finnegan, p. 18.

Chapter 14

1. *Uttarkandam*, 11. 35-52 in *Valmiki Ramayana*, Gita Press, Gorakhpur.
2. *Ibid.*, pp. 16, 25-46.
3. Swami Pramavananda, *Kailash Manasarovar* pp. 7, 18.
4. Charles Allen, *A Mountain in Tibet*, Andic Deutsch, London, 1982, p.26.
5. *Manaskhand*, 18.177, *A Portion of Skanda Purana*, ed. with glossary, etc. by Prof. Gopal Datt Pandey, Shri Nityananda Smarak Samiti, Varanasi, 1989.
6. Lama Anagarika Govinda, *The Way of the White Cloud*, p. 201.

Chapter 15

1. Choying Dorje, *Buddhism in Tibet*, translated for this book by Gyurme.
2. *Sabha Parva*, 52. 2-4, in *Mahabharata* Gita Press, Gorakhpur.
3. As described in Charles Allen, *A Mountain in Tibet*, Andic Deutsch, London, p. 144.
4. *Brahmanda Purana*, Translated and Annotated by Ganesh Vasudeo Tagore, Moti Lal Banarsi Das, 1983, Vol. I, 2.25. 20-40.
5. Quoted in Allen, p. 51.
6. A.P. Tiwary, geologist.

Chapter 16

1. A. Tom Grunfeld, *The Making of Modern Tibet*, Oxford University Press, 1987, p. 15.
2. John Snelling, *The Sacred Mountain*, East West Publications, London, 1983, p.15.

3. *Ibid.*
4. *Manaskhand,* 8.59, *A Portion of Skanda Purana,* ed. with glossary, etc. by Prof. Gopal Datt Pandey, Shri Nityananda Smarak Samiti, Varanasi, 1989.
5. Lama Anagarika Govinda, *The Way of the White Cloud,* p. 201.
6. Choying Dorje, *Buddhism in Tibet.*
7. Swami Pranavananda, *Kailash Manasarovar,* p. 23.

Chapter 17
1. Lama Anagarika Govinda, *The Way of the White Cloud,* p. 68.

Chapter 19
1. *Atisha* : *A Biography of the Renowned Buddhist Sage.* Translated from Tibetan Sources by Lama Thubten Kalsang et al., The Social Science Association Press of Thailand, Bangkok, 1974.
2. *Ibid.,* p. 47.
3. Jack Finnegan, *Tibet: A Dreamt of Image,* Tibet House, New Delhi, 1986, pp. 38-43.
4. *Ibid.,* p. 57.
5. *Ibid.,* p. 63.
6. David Snellgrove, pp. 129-31.
7. *Ibid.,* p. 146.
8. *Ibid.,* p. 147.
9. Jack Finnegan, *Tibet: A Dreamt of Image,* Tibet House, New Delhi, 1986, p. 114.
10. Olschak, Blache Co., Gansser, Augusto, Buhrer, Emil M., *People, Myths and Mountains of the Himalayas,* Motovun, Switzerland, 1987, p. 58.

Chapter 20
1. V.S. Agrawal, *Shiva Mahadeva,* Veda Academy, Varanasi 5, 1996, p. 29.
2. Stella Kramrisch, *The Presence of Shiva,* New Delhi: Oxford University Press, 1981, p. 284.
3. V.S. Agrawal, p. 17.
4. Pandit Ram Kinkar Upadhyaya, *Manas Manthan, Tritiya Ratna, Shiva Tattva,* (Hindi) Tulsi Anusandhana Kendra, Kanpur, 1983, p.62.
5. Stella Kramrisch, p. 171.
6. Ibid, p. 185.
7. Choying Dorje, *Tibetan Buddhism.*
8. Russel Johnson, and Kerry Moran, *The Sacred Mountain of Tibet* : *On Pilgrimage to Kailash,* Park Street Press, Vermont, p. 61.
9. *Devi Mahatmayam,* Gita Press, Gorakhpur, 2.30.
10. *Sadguru Swami Gangeswarananda ke Lekh tatha Upadesa* (Hindi) ed. by

Swami Govindananda Vedacarya (Sri Govindram Seumal, Bombay, 1965), p. 505.

Chapter 21

1. Charles Allen, *A Mountain in Tibet*, Andic Deutsch, London, p. 33.
2. Lama Anagarika Govinda, *The Way of the White Cloud,* p. 234.
3. A. Tom Grunfeld, *The Making of Modern Tibet*, Oxford University Press, 1987, p. 25.
4. Lama Anagarika Govinda, *The Way of the White Cloud,* p. 22.
5. Ibid, p. 23.
6. Narrated in Vijaya Ramaswamy, *Walking Naked: Women, Society and Spirituality in Southern India,* Indian Institute of Advanced Studies, Shimla, 1997, p. 130-31.
7. V.S. Agrawal, *Shiva Mahadeva,* p. 29.
8. Han Suyin, *Lhasa the Open City: A Journey to Tibet*, Jonathan Cape, London, 1977.
9. Quoted in John Snelling, *The Sacred Mountain,* p. 189.
10. Lama Anagarika Govinda, *The Way of the White Cloud,* p. 81.
11. David Snellgrove and Hugh Richardson, *A Cultural History of Tibet,* UBS, Delhi, 1968, p. 132.
12. Jack Finnegan, *Tibet: A Dreamt of Image,* p. 92.
13. David Snellgrove, *A Cultural History of Tibet,* p. 134.

Chapter 22

1. Lama Anagarika Govinda, *The Way of the White Cloud,* p. 68.
2. Swami Pranavananda, *Kailash-Manasarovar*, Published by Swami Pranavananda, 1949, Reprint 1983, pp. 64-68.

Chapter 23

1. Stella Kramrisch, *The Presence of Shiva,* p. 188.
2. *Ibid.*, p. 433.
3. V.S. Agrawal, *Shiva Mahadeva,* p. 4.
4. Quoted in John Snelling, *The Sacred Mountain*, East West Publications, London, 1983, p. 191.

Bibliography

Agrawal, Vasudeva S., *Siva Mahadeva, The Great God: An Exposition of the Symbolism of Siva* (Veda Academy, Varanasi – 5, 1966).

Evans-Wentz, W.Y., *Tibet's Great Yogi Milarepa: A Biography from the Tibetan* (OUP, 1951).

Finnegan, Jack, *Tibet: A Dreamt of Image* (Tibet House, New Delhi, 1986).

Govinda, Lama Anagarika, *The Way of the White Cloud: A Buddhist Pilgrim in Tibet* (B.I. Publications, Bombay, 1977).

Harrer, Heinrich, *Return to Tibet* (George Weidenfeld & Nicolson, London, 1984).

Heim, Arnold and Gansser, August, *The Throne of the Gods: An Account of the First Swiss Expedition to the Himalayas*, translated by Eden and Cedar Paul (Book Faith India, Delhi, 1994).

Johnson, Russel and Moran, Kerry, *The Sacred Mountain of Tibet: On Pilgrimage to Kailas* (Park Street Press, Rochester, Vermont, 1989).

Kramrisch, Stella, *The Presence of Siva* (OUP, 1981).

Lama Thubten Kalsang *et alia*, *Atisha: A Biography of the Renowned Buddhist Sage, Translated from Tibetan Sources* (The Social Science Association Press of Thailand, Bangkok, 1974).

Macdonald, David, *Cultural Heritage of Tibet* (Light and Life Publishers, New Delhi, n.d.).

Mehra, Parshottam, *The Younghusband Expedition: An Interpretation* (Asia Publishing House, New Delhi, 1968).

Olschak, Blanche C., Gansser, Augusto, Buhrer, Emil M., *People, Myths and Mountains of the Himalayas* (Facts of File Publications, N.Y., 1987).

Poornalingam, M.S., *Ravana the Great* (Solden and Co., Printers, Madras) Publisher and date not available.

Singh, Jaideva, *Siva Sutras: The Yoga of Supreme Identity* (Motilal Banarsidass, New Delhi, 1979).

Snellgrove, David, and Richardson, Hugh, *A Cultural History of Tibet* (UBS, Delhi, 1968).

Snelling, John, *The Sacred Mountain: Travellers and Pilgrims at Mount Kailas in Western Tibet, and the Great Universal Symbol of the Sacred Mountain* (East West Publications, London, 1983).

Suyin, Han, *Lhasa the Open City: A Journey to Tibet* (Jonathan Cape, London, 1977).

Swami Govindananda Vedantacharya, ed., *Sadguru Swami Gangesvarananda ke lekh tatha Upadesa*, no.4 (Sri Govindram Seumal, Bombay, 1965).

Swami Krishnananda, *Spiritual Import of Religious Festivals* (The Divine Life Society, Rishikesh, 1982).

Swami Pranavananda, *Kailas Manasarovar*, 2nd edition (Swami Pranavananda, New Delhi, 1983).

Swami Sivananda, *Lord Siva and His Worship* (Yoga Vedanta Forest Academy Press, Rishikesh, 1962).

Swami Venkatesananda, *The Cosmic Dance* (Chiltern Yoga Trust, Mauritius, 1986).

Upadhyaya, Pandit Ram Kinkar, *Manas Manthan: Siva Tattva, Trittiya Ratna In the Image of Man* (Vikas Publishing House Pvt Ltd.).

Welbon, Guy R. and Yocum Glenn E., ed., *Religious Festivals in South India and Sri Lanka* (Manohar, New Delhi, 1962).

Brahmanda Purana, Tr. and Annotated Ganesh Vasdeo Tagare (Motilal Banarsi Dass, 1983).

Manas Khanda: A portion of the Skandapurana, ed. with glossary, etc. by Prof. Gopal Datt Pandey (Shri Nityananda Smarak Samiti, Varanasi, 1989).

Markandeya Purana, translated with notes by F. Eden Pargiter (The Asiatic Society, Calcutta, 1904).

Mahabharat (Gita Press, Gorakhpur).

Srimad Bhagavata Mahapurana, Rendered into English by C.L. Goswami (Gita Press, Gorakhpur).

Valmiki Ramayana, Gita Press, Gorakhpur.

Visnu Purana, Gita Press, Gorakhpur.